V. DUNCAN.

CASSELL CARAVEL BOOKS

A CASSELL CARAVEL BOOK

RUSSIA IN REVOLUTION

By the Editors of
HORIZON MAGAZINE

Author
E. M. HALLIDAY

In consultation with
CYRIL E. BLACK
Professor of History, Princeton University

Cassell · London

Trademark CARAVEL registered United States Patent Office
First published in Great Britain 1968
Printed and bound in Italy by Arnoldo Mondadori Editore
S.B.N. 304 93218 3

FOREWORD

The turbulent events that overtook Russia in 1917 are often called one of history's great turning points. A corrupt, outdated, and careworn autocracy—that of the three-hundred-year-old Romanov dynasty—was overthrown in March of that year by a spontaneous uprising of Russia's long-oppressed masses. During the next few months Alexander Kerensky and other forward-looking liberals of the Provisional Government attempted to give Russia its first taste of freedom. But the continuing hardships of World War I and the pressure of a radical minority, Lenin's Bolsheviks, proved too much for them. In the relatively bloodless *coup d'état* of November 7, Lenin and his associates seized control of the state.

To understand and appreciate these historic events, one must look back—as the author of the following narrative does—to the nineteenth-century origins of Russian revolutionary thought, to the abortive uprising of 1905 and the subsequent, short-lived reforms, and to the devastating war with Germany that caused an empire to stagger. The events can be illuminated also by a study of such personalities as the ineffectual Nicholas and his domineering wife, Alexandra, the sinister Rasputin and his aristocratic murderer Prince Yusupov, and—most importantly—the two men from nearly identical backgrounds who took such different paths, Kerensky and Lenin. Painters, cartoonists, and photographers of many lands were fascinated and disturbed by revolutionary Russia, and the wide variety of works reproduced here reflects their interest.

The Communists, as Russia's new Bolshevik leaders styled themselves in early 1918, confidently expected the workers and peasants of other lands to follow their example by setting up similar governments. But the majority of countries that have taken the road to Communism in the last half-century have been forced to do so by Russian armies. In Russia itself, the people's government envisioned by Lenin became the cruel dictatorship of Joseph Stalin. The fiftieth anniversary celebrated by the Soviet Union in November, 1967, honors the dramatic insurrection that has nevertheless proved to be but one incident in the long—and perhaps continuing—struggle of a troubled people for a better way of life.

THE EDITORS

Through the arch at left to the Winter Palace beyond, Bolshevik soldiers passed on their way to overthrow the Provisional Government. Today the Palace halls echo with the footsteps of tourists come to see the famous Hermitage art collection, and the former Petrograd is called Leningrad.

RIGHT: *A Communist poster of the 1920's shows a Red Army soldier, triumphant in Russia, looking for new conquests in Europe.*

COVER: *Carrying the red flag of revolution, a truckload of rebels approaches Moscow's Kremlin.*

FRONT ENDSHEET: *E. B. Lintott, an eyewitness to Russia's revolution, painted a 1918 demonstration.*

TITLE PAGE: *Soviet Russia's hammer and sickle emblem represents the nation's workers and farmers.*

BACK ENDSHEET: *Hailing the end of czarism, soldiers march across Petrograd in a 1917 parade supporting Kerensky's government.*

BACK COVER: *The dynamic leader of the 1917 Bolshevik insurrection, Lenin, appears in his role as a fiery, crowd-swaying orator.*

CONTENTS

I

Снятие орлов и царских портретов 5 марта 1917 г.

THE END OF CZARISM

On March 9, 1917, a mounted Cossack winked at a striking workman as he galloped past him down a street in Petrograd, the capital of Imperial Russia. It may have been the most significant wink in modern history. It meant that Czar Nicholas II's best soldiers were going to let him down when the crucial moment came to suppress the mobs of rebellious workers who roamed the city on that Friday morning—the last Friday that a czar would ever sit on the Russian throne.

The odd thing about the revolution that abruptly ended three hundred years of rule by the House of Romanov was that nobody planned it—and therefore nobody expected it just when it happened or foresaw just how it would unfold.

By the first weeks of 1917 it was already clear to nearly everyone, except perhaps the Czar and his wife, the Czarina Alexandra, that the hundreds of thousands of factory workers in Petrograd were in a dangerously belligerent mood. Labor strikes were increasing in number and intensity. For two and a half years the nation had been at war with Germany, and most people were sick of it. Yet a revolution that stood any chance of success did not seem likely. The police of the capital city had been reinforced by a garrison of about 160,000 soldiers, all well armed, and an elaborate plan had been designed for systematically putting down any mass movement of striking workers that might threaten serious trouble. As for the workers, despite their disgust with the war and the government, despite their bitter discontent with the scarcity and cost of food and fuel, they did not consciously feel that the time was ripe for a violent overthrow of the regime. Yet active revolutionaries had infiltrated the manfacturing plants of Petrograd. It had always been assumed that when the long-awaited revolu-

An eyewitness to the tumultuous events in revolutionary Russia, I. Vladimirov, painted the water color at left in March, 1917. To the cheers of their comrades, soldiers carry a portrait of Czar Nicholas II to a bonfire.

11

tion came, it would be spearheaded by such agitators, who would have planned the whole thing step by step.

Many revolutionary leaders, however, were absent in March, 1917. This was most notably true of the Communists, or Social Democrats, as they were then called. Lenin, their guiding genius, was in Switzerland, feeling very unhopeful about the chances of a revolution in Russia. Leon Trotsky, soon to become his chief lieutenant, was in New York City, where he helped edit a revolutionary newspaper. Joseph Stalin, the young man who one day would be the Communist dictator, was in exile in Siberia. Although some other revolutionaries of distinction were present, they were, so to speak, absent in mind: they failed to estimate correctly the mood of the people and—especially—the mood of the soldiers.

A good example was Alexander Kerensky, a brilliant young labor leader and member of the Duma, or legislative council. At the end of February he was making bold speeches before that body suggesting that removal of Nicholas II—"by terrorist methods if there is no other way"—would solve the national problem; he was not thinking in terms of mass revolution. "I hope that Duma man Kedrinsky," wrote the Czarina to the Czar, getting the name wrong, "will be hung for his horrible speeches—it is necessary and it will be an example."

But neither assassinating Czar Nicholas nor hanging men like Kerensky was the solution that history had in store for Russia's plight.

On the cold Thursday morning of March 8,* there were some disturbances in the workers' sections of Petrograd—a number of women who had been waiting in long lines in front of bakeries grew angry when they were told there was no more bread. That same morning the women workers of several Petrograd textile plants went out on strike; and they were soon followed by thousands of men from the metal factories. The discontented workers began a demonstration, carrying banners that said "We want bread." A crowd formed around them, and soon there were speeches on street corners, choruses of the French revolutionary song and national anthem, the Marseillaise—sung in Russian, of course—and shouts of "Down with the war" in addition

*In 1917 Russia was still using the Julian calendar, thirteen days behind the Gregorian calendar used elsewhere in Europe at the time and universally today. Thus, according to the "Old Style" Russian calendar, the revolution began on February 23, and the overthrow of the czarist regime is sometimes referred to as the February revolution.

to "We want bread." Police reserves were called out to keep things in hand, but so far there was little violence, although occasionally someone would pick up a chunk of ice from the snow-covered streets and hurl it at a passing officer.

By the morning of March 9, the streets of the city were jammed with huge crowds of striking workers—estimated at close to 200,000, half Petrograd's entire industrial force. It was apparent that a massive strike was developing, and the authorities nervously called out the Cossacks.

The Cossacks, on their big horses and carrying their sabers, were the traditional instrument of the Russian monarchy for punishing troublesome citizens. They enjoyed special privileges in the army, and many a time they had shown how fiercely and efficiently they could carry out the Czar's orders. On March 9, 1917, they pranced their horses into the crowds as usual or broke into a galloping charge when ordered to do so by their officers. But the crowds of workers noticed a difference: the Cossacks were being careful with their sabers, were not touching their firearms, and looked down on the upturned faces with a surprising lack of ferocity. Then came the wink that was to become famous; shortly thereafter the word flashed around that a Cossack patrol had actually driven off some policemen who were beating up workers on a street corner. The next time a troop of Cossacks galloped through a crowd, they were greeted with hurrahs, as if they were putting on a show.

The military commander of Petrograd was baffled; but there seemed to be nothing to do but call out more soldiers. Most of the infantrymen, however, turned out to be even more inclined than the Cossacks to favor the people: they carried their bayoneted rifles at a harmless angle, and many of them started up friendly conversations with the strikers. It must be realized that most of these soldiers were not professionals but were peasants who had been forced from their villages to replace brothers and cousins already killed or wounded in the war. They hated it and naturally felt much sympathy for a crowd of fellow citizens whose only demands seemed to be for bread and an end to the war.

By March 10 Petrograd was in a seething uproar. The streetcars had stopped running, and thousands of shop clerks and students had joined the masses of striking workers. The temperature was well below zero: great clouds of steam puffed from horses' nostrils and rose from the shouting and singing crowds.

And now the police started shooting. But instead of running for their homes, the crowds surged forward, disarmed

OVERLEAF: *The revolution that overtook Nicholas in 1917 was foreshadowed in this 1905 American cartoon. Wolves symbolizing rebellious forces pursue the Czar's runaway troika. To avoid Death lurking in the trees, he considers a sacrifice of the baby Autocracy.*

Puck, APRIL 5, 1905

Happy Petrograd citizens rummage among heaps of partly destroyed police archives taken from a looted government building. Secret files kept on many Russians had been used by the czarist regime to suppress opposition forces.

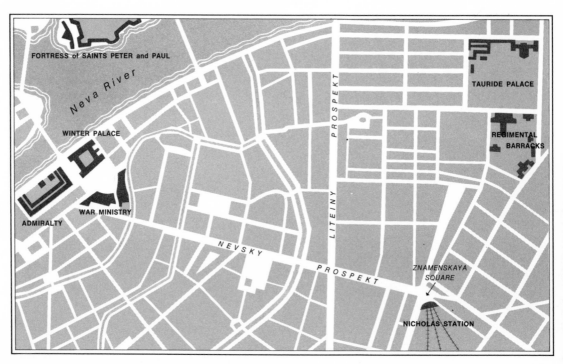

Most of the events of the March revolution were enacted in this central section of Petrograd. Violence erupted several times at Znamenskaya Square, as workers attempted to march up broad Nevsky Prospekt toward government headquarters at the Admiralty and Winter Palace. The scene of action was later to shift to the Tauride Palace, where members of the dissolved Duma and committees of revolutionary soldiers and workers were rivals for power.

16

and killed some of the policemen, and wrecked police stations in the workers' districts. In one incident that afternoon, in Znamenskaya Square, a Cossack was said to have killed a policeman. Late into the night shots could be heard, and fires burned fitfully where station houses had been set to flame. The people of Petrograd slept badly that night: the whole situation seemed obscure and uncertain; nobody knew for sure what was happening. It was rumored that on the following day the soldiers would be ordered to shoot anyone who appeared on the streets.

On Sunday morning, March 11, things seemed to have quieted down—but only for a little while. Soon the crowds of workers were out again, pushing across the Neva River bridges into the main part of Petrograd or crossing on the snow-covered ice. Again trouble developed at Znamenskaya Square. One unit of soldiers, firing into a crowd, killed forty demonstrators and wounded another forty. This brutal act was heatedly discussed by the soldiers in their barracks that night.

What happened the next morning, Monday, marked the true pivot of the revolution. In several parts of the city, and especially in the workers' districts, the soldiers began to help the people against the police. Soon entire regiments had broken up and were mingling freely with the workers, even passing out weapons to them from their barracks. Now the terrified police were being cornered and shot like rabbits; suddenly they became difficult to find. To be caught in a policeman's uniform meant death; and the same thing was true for army officers who tried to discipline their men instead of joining the revolution.

During this amazing series of happenings the members of the Russian ruling class from the Czar on down to the Duma were quite unable to react fast enough to keep up with the swift developments.

After a visit at the Imperial Palace outside Petrograd the Czar, with extraordinarily bad timing, had left for the military front on the very day that the revolution started. He knew that the atmosphere in the city was explosive, but perhaps for that very reason he longed to get back to the quiet of his headquarters, which was well behind the firing line. "My brain is resting here," he wrote to his wife, "no Ministers, no troublesome questions demanding thought." And, like Nero, who is said to have fiddled while Rome burned, he noted: "I shall take up dominoes again in my spare time." He was soon going to have more time for dominoes than he ever dreamed of.

Raising their sabers and rifles, soldiers who have deserted to the Revolution pose under a banner marked "Down with Monarchy."

The Czar's ministers and the leading members of the Duma were startled and apprehensive as they watched the demonstrations of March 8 to March 11. They understood that a tremendous revolutionary force was erupting like a volcano, and there seemed to be little possibility of controlling it. Agitated telegrams were sent to the Czar, but his reactions were not helpful. On Saturday, March 10, he telegraphed the military commander at Petrograd: "I command you to suppress from tomorrow all disorders on the streets of the capital, which are impermissible at a time when the fatherland is carrying on a difficult war with Germany." The harassed commander prepared a proclamation to carry out the Czar's order but could not find enough glue to post it on city streets.

By Monday, March 12, then, the tide of the revolution was at the full, and there would be no stopping it. The few companies of soldiers still under the command of the authorities were unreliable: when they were dispatched in patrols to form a new line of resistance against the rebellion, they simply dissolved into the crowds, and their weapons became part of the revolutionary arsenal.

By this time, armored cars flying the red flag of socialism were cruising the streets, and the workers had taken over many machine guns. The people sensed that victory was on their side, and the excitement was keen. A journalist who was making his way across the turbulent city reported that cars and trucks kept going by, "in which soldiers, workers, students, and young women, some wearing arm-bands, were sitting or standing. God knows where all these came from, where they were rushing to, or with what purpose! But all these passengers were extremely excited, shouting and waving their arms, scarcely aware of what they were doing." Everyone talked eagerly to everyone else, acquainted or not, trying to pick up information about the latest developments. Rumors flew, but there was one thing that all were sure of: the old days were over, and something new was about to begin.

Now the focus of the rebellion became the Tauride Palace, which held the Duma's meeting halls. The legislative body had been suspended by order of the Czar, but some of the leaders favored ignoring the decree. On Monday morning the Duma members gathered at the Tauride to debate what their role ought to be. "I don't want to revolt," M. V. Rodzianko, the Duma president, protested; and no doubt he expressed the feeling of the majority of his colleagues. But one of the members of the Duma quickly said:

As fighting rages in Petrograd pamphlets advocating change are distributed to peaceful, news-hungry throngs in a Moscow street

"We have got to take charge. If we don't, others will."

It was obvious to the Duma leaders that if any connections at all were going to be maintained with the old government, some kind of definite move would have to be made. Therefore, they hastily established the Temporary Committee of the Duma. The purpose of the committee, they announced, was to try to give some shape to the chaotic state of affairs in Petrograd—not to suppress the revolution (it was in any case too late for that), but to bring some order into its results.

Just a few hours later another meeting was going on in the same Tauride Palace. There a kind of improvised "staff" of the unplanned revolution was belatedly set up: some of the labor leaders, remembering the days of an earlier attempt at revolution in 1905, decided to re-establish a "Soviet of Workers' Deputies." They named themselves as a temporary "Executive Committee of the Soviet." ("Soviet" in Russian means "council.") Delegates were to be elected immediately to the Soviet from all the local factories and also from the numerous military units that had now come over to the side of the revolution. The first meeting of the

Ankle-deep in snow, the soldiers at left pose behind a Petrograd street barricade, as curious bystanders peer from the background. One of the nearly buried cannons still flies its revolutionary red flag.

OVERLEAF: *Crowds, mostly of armed soldiers, spill across the broad, snow-packed expanse of the capital's principal boulevard, Nevsky Prospekt. This photograph from a French magazine was one of the first revolutionary scenes published outside Russia.*
L'Illustration

Soviet was to be held in the Tauride Palace that very night, March 12.

By late afternoon of that day, the delegates to the Soviet, plus large groups of their supporters, as well as the merely curious—a great mixed crowd of workers, soldiers, and students—were milling in and about the Tauride. The meeting began that evening, and after a long series of excited "reports" from soldier delegates—many of them still carrying their rifles—the delegates began to elect committees to deal with the most pressing problems of bringing order back to Petrograd.

So it was that almost from the beginning of the great Russian Revolution two rival power centers were created. On the one hand was the Soviet of Workers' and Soldiers' Deputies (as it was now to be called), with its Executive Committee dominated by socialist labor leaders who insisted that Russia must become a republic. On the other

Members of the old Imperial Duma tried to keep up with the turbulent events already passing them by. Here M. V. Rodzianko (seated, extreme right), president of the dissolved legislative council, confers with soon-to-be-forgotten colleagues. Standing behind him is a brooding Alexander Kerensky, who came to dominate the Provisional Government these men were then in the process of forming.

hand there was the Temporary Committee of the Duma, composed of liberal and moderately conservative politicians who placed their hands on the torch of revolution with a good deal of reluctance. Many of them would have preferred to have the nation become a constitutional monarchy, still with a czar, but one whose dictatorial powers would be almost entirely taken away. They felt that such a government would be more likely to guarantee the property rights of the middle-class businessmen and upper-class landowners whom they represented.

There was one link between the two power centers—Alexander Kerensky, who was a member of both committees. His role, unavoidably, was going to be a highly important one, and he recognized it from the first. A man who was able to give the impression of great self-assurance in a crisis, he strode briskly through the halls of the Tauride Palace. He made dozens of speeches, ordered excited workers not to harm any of the members of the Czar's Council of Ministers who had been rounded up and brought in as prisoners, and sent out detachments of soldiers to guard the railroad stations in case czarist troops were moved in from outside the city. There were a hundred other important things to be done, and Kerensky tried to keep a finger on all of them—a difficult feat, in view of the number of fingers nature has allotted to one man.

What of the Czar? He had not yet given up his throne, yet without his knowing it, history already had passed him by. On the morning of Tuesday, March 13, a member of the Soviet Executive Committee, who, like many others, had spent the night curled up on his overcoat on the floor of the Tauride Palace, woke up to the grunts of a couple of soldiers who were poking at a big painting with their bayonets. It was a portrait of Nicholas II, and they were cutting the picture out of the frame to the accompaniment of very uncomplimentary remarks.

Nicholas himself, on that morning, was on his private train, trying to get back to his palace at Tsarskoe Selo, a suburb of Petrograd. He wanted to be with his family, come what might. The railroad lines leading to Petrograd, however, had been taken over by rebels, and it soon became clear that they would interfere with the progress of the imperial train. Nicholas therefore turned aside and went to the headquarters of one of his generals, at a place called Pskov, arriving on the evening of Wednesday, March 14. The next day he was informed that it was the opinion not only of the Temporary Committee of the Duma, but also of the generals in command of all the fighting fronts, that he must abdicate the throne.

The Czar took this news quite calmly, almost as if emperors were asked to give up their crowns every day. Two members of the Duma arrived from Petrograd to receive Nicholas' signed abdication, and he listened with a look of patient boredom while they explained at length the necessity for this step. The only change he insisted on was that the throne should not go to his son (a boy of twelve in delicate health) but to his brother, the Grand Duke Michael.

The two Duma members left for Petrograd on the evening of Thursday, March 15, taking the abdication paper with them, and Nicholas wrote in his diary, before going to bed in his private car: ". . . To save Russia and keep the army at the front, I decided upon this step . . . At 1 o'clock in the morning I left Pskov with heavy feelings; around me treason, cowardice, deceit."

The rebellious residents of Petrograd wasted no time in removing signs of the discredited czarist regime. Above right, a man on a ladder pries loose an imperial insignia from a building front. The citizens and soldiers at left are warming themselves near a fire of junked royal signs and emblems.

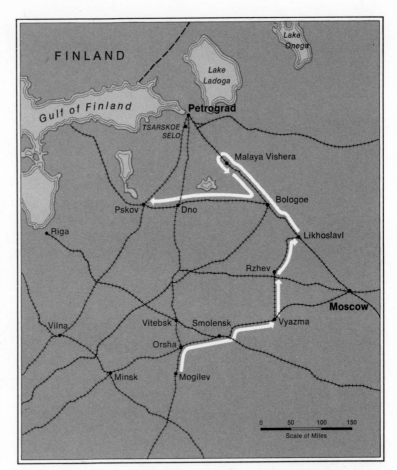

With his empire collapsing in revolution, Nicholas vainly attempted to reach his family at Tsarskoe Selo. On the map at right is his route from G.H.Q. at Mogilev. Leaving more direct routes open for the passage of troops to quell the Petrograd uprising, Nicholas' royal train headed east and then north as far as Malaya Vishera, where it was blocked by hostile forces. Backtracking, he went to Pskov, where he abdicated the throne.

Evidently, however, his heavy feelings were soon lightened by the reflection that the responsibilities of czardom, which he had always disliked, had now been lifted from his shoulders as if by a miracle. "I had a long and sound sleep," the diary entry for the next day reads. ". . . Sunshine and frost. . . . I read much of Julius Caesar." A week later he was placed in captivity in his own home at Tsarskoe Selo, along with his beloved wife, Alexandra. Stifling her burning indignation at what had happened to her husband, the Czarina busied herself with her children. All of them were sick with measles.

Back at the Tauride Palace in Petrograd the events of the revolution had been plunging ahead. On March 15 the Temporary Committee of the Duma had announced, by agreement with the Petrograd Soviet, the formation of a Provisional Government (composed largely of the same group of men) that would rule the country until a national "constituent assembly" could meet. Such an assembly

5665

26

would have representatives from the entire country, and they would decide exactly what kind of nation Russia would now become. One thing was already certain: it would not be a monarchy, under either the Grand Duke Michael or anyone else. The Grand Duke, in fact, seeing how things were going, judiciously abdicated the throne without ever having occupied it.

Meanwhile it was clear that the Soviet of Workers' and Soldiers' Deputies was going to act as a kind of unofficial congress or parliament: very little could be accomplished by the Provisional Government without its approval. For example, on March 14 the Soviet issued to the soldiers of the Petrograd garrison "Order No. 1," which soon became famous. It was interpreted as an order to "democratize" the army; soldiers were to have the same rights as other citizens except when actually performing military duties; there was to be no more off-duty saluting; all weapons were to be controlled by the enlisted men, not the officers. Furthermore, orders issued by the Duma military commission "should be carried out only in those cases where they do not contradict the orders of the Soviet of Workers' and Soldiers' Deputies." It has been said that Order No. 1 marked the start of a long struggle between the Provisional Government and the Soviet, a conflict that would finally be settled only by a second revolution, some eight months later —the Communist revolution of November, 1917.

For the time being, however, a kind of peace had descended on Russia. An enormous mountain of difficult problems had to be immediately confronted, but at least the revolution that so many had dreamed of for so many decades, the revolution that would free Russia from czarism, had actually taken place—and with far less violence and bloodshed than anyone could have anticipated.

Fresh snow had fallen. Walking through the now nearly empty streets of Petrograd, a member of the Soviet Executive Committee felt a sense of intense elation despite his fatigue. "I was walking," he wrote later, "through a free city of the new Russia. . . . Where was Czarism? It was gone. It had crumbled away in an instant. Three centuries to build it up, and three days for it to vanish."

Emperor without an empire, a forlorn Nicholas II sits on a stump at Tsarskoe Selo, as soldiers of the Provisional Government stand guard. The deposed ruler of millions was respectfully treated by his captors, who allowed him such invigorating chores as chopping wood and shoveling snow.

II

WHAT NICHOLAS LOST

When Nicholas II was toppled from his throne by the Revolution in March, 1917, he lost what in many ways was the most powerful monarchy in the world. Russia's vast geographical extent (almost as large as all of North America), her huge population (about 148 million in 1917), and her abundant natural resources were the basis of this power—but the peculiar character of czarist rule was the key to it.

In spite of rapid industrialization from the 1880's to the outbreak of World War I in 1914, Russia remained primarily an agricultural nation. Well over eighty per cent of her population was rural. Until 1861 the vast Russian farmlands were tilled by millions of serfs—that is, peasants who "went with the land" and were actually the property of the noble landlords, like cattle or sheep. The serfs, of course, had no voice in how the great empire was run. As long as the czar could count on the loyal support of his nobles, he was a true autocrat—a monarch whose authority was absolute. The laws of the realm were what he wanted them to be.

On top of that, however, the Russian government itself owned nearly half the peasants. Huge tracts of land were farmed for the benefit of the Russian state and the czar's private treasury. The government was also in charge of extensive enterprises that in the United States and Western Europe would have been left largely in private hands. It owned and operated many industrial plants, as well as the railroads and all other communications; it supported and controlled the Russian Orthodox Church, the official state church, and all schools and universities; it also censored all publications. When to all this is added the czar's command of an enormous army and the navy, it can be seen

In the savage cartoon opposite, Russia's chained masses carry a litter representing the state over the bones of their predecessors. A maniacal czar listens to an evil priest, as a capitalist cracks a whip over the bearers.

Nicholas I

Alexander II

that long before the revolutionary changes of the twentieth century, Russians were used to having the state hover over their lives in "big brother" fashion.

Much of Russian history is heavy with a sense of pressure—the pressure of the great, sullen masses of underprivileged peasants whose frustrated human desires might at some time break out into the open. From time to time there actually were ferocious rebellions, touched off when the ordinarily lethargic serfs were aroused by intolerable conditions to lash out in protest against their masters and the czar. Oddly, the leaders of such rebellions often became romantic figures even in the eyes of the aristocrats, as if the idea of a violent blow for freedom appealed to the Russian spirit regardless of one's particular social status.

It was not until the early nineteenth century, however, that there was a revolt based on any plan of reforming the Russian government. Significantly, it was organized by a group of young nobles, rather than by anyone from the underprivileged classes. In December, 1825, the succession of Czar Nicholas I to the throne was resisted by some young army officers and intellectuals. The movement was quickly crushed: Nicholas had five of the conspirators executed and sent many others to exile in Siberia. But the Decembrists, as they were called, were fondly remembered by Russians who longed for a freer society.

Among the aims of the Decembrists had been the abolition of serfdom and the setting up of a constitutional government. For nearly a century educated Russians—which meant, largely, the nobility—would be divided among those who supported the czar as an all-powerful dictator; those who sought moderate reform that would make the czar a constitutional monarch like the king of England; and those who wished to overthrow the government altogether.

Alexander II, the son of Nicholas I, aroused much hope among his people, for he decreed the emancipation of the serfs six years after he came to the throne in 1855. Yet, as it worked out, few of the liberated peasants were much more contented afterward than they had been before. They no longer were the property of the landlords, but the amount of land most of them held was not sufficient to yield a decent life to their families. This was partly because of the steady growth of Russia's peasant population, partly because of their primitive, inefficient farming methods, and partly because of complicated legal requirements on how their land was to be held. The "peasant question," as it was called, was not solved by emancipation.

Besides bringing an end to serfdom, Alexander took other steps toward modernizing the heavy and backward social structure of his country. A system of local self-government was instituted—the *zemstvos*, or county councils, whose members were elected by the people. Other reforms soon followed. Schools, hospitals, and roads were improved and rapidly increased in number; newer methods of agriculture were introduced; censorship of newspapers and books was eased somewhat; and trial by jury was established to give accused persons a greater chance for justice. The national government continued to play a big role in Russian society, however—in some respects an even bigger role than it had played prior to Alexander's reforms.

In any case, Alexander lived to regret many of those reforms. It must have seemed to him that people were ungrateful. Revolutionary groups, instead of fading away,

Regiments hostile to Nicholas I demonstrated in a St. Petersburg square on December 26, 1825. In the water color below, frenzied crowds hail the revolt, stamped out the same day by the new Czar.

A contemporary engraving shows Alexander II leaving his carriage to aid a wounded Cossack, as the assassin hurls another bomb. "To the palace, to die there," the wounded Czar ordered his driver.

were stimulated by the gains already made to demand much more radical changes. Among the most active and numerous of the reformers were the Narodniks (literally, "populists"), most of them students, who wished to turn the government over to the people in a form of socialism. They came to idealize the peasant and make him the focus of all their reform efforts.

In a movement of the early 1870's, Narodniks went to the people almost like missionaries, hoping to arouse the peasants to a revolution that would overthrow the czarist autocracy. Most peasants, however, were not ready for such a message and suspiciously regarded the Narodniks as troublesome "outsiders." The program was not a success.

In desperation, some of the Narodniks formed a secret organization called The People's Will, with "cells" that met regularly to plan acts of terror. Many such plans were boldly carried out: trains were dynamited, officials were assassinated, government buildings were bombed. There were several unsuccessful attempts on the Czar's life. Then, in March, 1881, as Alexander rode through St. Petersburg (Petrograd), a member of The People's Will tossed a bomb at his coach. Two Cossack guards fell to the ground, and the Czar leaped out to help them—just in time to meet a second explosion. He died an hour and a half later from his wounds. Five young members of The People's Will, including Sophie Perovskaya, the daughter of a prominent government official, were hanged for the assassination.

Alexander II, only a few hours before his sudden death, had approved a plan for a "consultative council" that would have given the public some voice in national affairs. The shock of the assassination brought an end to that. His son, Alexander III, turned his attention instead to expanding the network of his secret police in order to counteract further terrorism. His thirteen-year reign was an almost uninterrupted series of repressions, even though it was a period of great national progress for Russia in terms of industrial development and railroad building. One important result was that slowly but surely the segment of Russia's population engaged in factory work and other nonagricultural labor was growing.

A plot to kill Alexander III was nipped in the bud in 1887, and one of the executed leaders was Alexander Ulyanov. This young revolutionary had a seventeen-year-old brother named Vladimir Ilyich. He was a bright and studious boy with an intense personality, and he was soon to become a political agitator himself. Like most Russian revolutionaries of the far left, young Ulyanov chose an alias—one that would later become famous in the Russian Revolution: Lenin.

Quite unexpectedly, Alexander III died of a bronchial infection in 1894. Nicholas II, the next czar—and destined to be the last—possessed a character very different from that of his father. Both of them were handsome and well built, but there the resemblance ended. The father, Alexander III, had exactly the temperament of an autocrat: he was imperious in manner, sure of his feelings and ideas, quick to make hard and fast decisions, merciless toward anyone who crossed his will. Nearly everything he said was in the form of a command, and his commands were obeyed without question.

Nicholas—perhaps because he spent his boyhood in the shadow of this overwhelming father—was by contrast polite, quiet, often unsure of his opinion and likely to change it abruptly under pressure. He found disagreement of any kind unpleasant and always tried to avoid arguments. He charmed everyone—"a spirit of good will radiated brightly from him," said one of his government ministers, one who, in fact, was not fond of him. Yet this charm could be deceptive; for example, he would sometimes dismiss an aston-

Burly, domineering Alexander III poses with members of his family. Behind the bearded Czar is his eldest son, the future Nicholas II. Alexander and England's Edward VII were married to sisters.

ished official the morning after having entertained him in the imperial palace with every show of affection.

The truth is that Nicholas was not cut out to be an autocratic ruler. He might have made a good king of England, like his first cousin George V, whom he so much resembled. A strong prime minister and an independent parliament were the sort of guides he needed. But in Russia, where everything depended on the decision of the emperor, he was fated to be a failure; and he seemed to sense this himself. Although as czar he dutifully attended to his obliga-

tions, he lived for the hours when he could be away from official functions altogether, to play with his children, take tea with his wife, or go outdoors for one of the many sports he enjoyed, such as swimming or hunting.

As historical luck would have it, this amiable individual fell in love, when still very young, with a girl whose personality was destined to make his weaknesses count more rather than less. Princess Alix of Hesse-Darmstadt was a German by birth, but she had been brought up from the age of six by her grandmother, Queen Victoria of Eng-

In the sanctuary of Moscow's ornate Cathedral of the Assumption a metropolitan of the Russian Orthodox Church anoints Nicholas II following his coronation. Proudly watching her husband at the right is the lovely new Czarina. This 1897 water color by V. Serov was painted for a royal album.

35

land. As might have been expected, her notions of etiquette, of morality, and of religion were "Victorian" to the highest degree—that is to say, rigid and narrow, but rooted in very strong convictions. The education her tutors gave her was sketchy on the side of information and reasoning; any high school graduate today understands a good deal more about the world than this elegant princess did when, as a seventeen-year-old, she spent six weeks in St. Petersburg and the twenty-one-year-old Nicholas fell head over heels in love with her.

Alix was a pretty girl, but to most members of the Russian court and St. Petersburg society her charm was a secret that only Nicholas grasped. Despite a stubborn will, she was outwardly shy; besides, at first she spoke no Russian. (She and Nicholas carried on their courtship in English; and ever afterward this was to be the language of their intimate life together.) Then there was the obstacle of her religion: she had been raised in the Church of England, and the idea of converting to the strange rites of the Russian Orthodox faith at first repelled her.

Once she had made the decision, however, Alix embraced her new creed with fervent enthusiasm. She seemed to feel that total devotion to the Russian form of Christianity would make up for her German birth, her English upbringing, and her natural awkwardness with everything else that was Russian; besides, according to the Orthodox Church, the Czar was directly anointed by God as the leader of his people. This anointed man became her own beloved husband and before long the father of her children, and her religious feelings tended to get tangled up with her family loyalty.

Nicholas' marriage to Alix followed a few weeks after his father's death in 1894. His coronation, for which elaborate preparations were necessary, had to wait until May, 1896. This great event at Russia's old capital, Moscow, was marked by two accidents that must have struck millions of Russians as bad omens; they certainly so struck the Czarina, for she proved early to be a very superstitious woman.

During the coronation ceremony a St. Andrew's Cross that Nicholas was wearing fell unaccountably to the floor. A few hours later, through unbelievable mismanagement

Looking every inch the proper Victorian couple they were, Alexandra and Nicholas strike the pose considered standard for late-nineteenth-century wedding portraits—she sitting primly, he standing stiffly nonchalant.

37

on the part of police authorities, there was a horrible panic in a field tightly crowded with peasants who had come to Moscow to see the new Czar. It was customary on such an occasion to distribute small presents to the poor; and somehow the rumor started that there were not enough gifts to go around. The crowd surged forward, some wooden covers over several deep ditches gave way, and an estimated two thousand were crushed to death or suffocated in the trample. Whether because he failed to understand what had happened or because of his tendency to look the other way from anything unpleasant, the newly crowned Czar made matters worse by proceeding calmly to the French ambassador's ball, where the food, wine, music, and dancing were brilliant. People began talking of the Czar's birth on the feast of St. Job as a further omen that he too would be beset with troubles sent from God.

Nicholas revered his father's memory, and this gave rise to a fatal paradox. Unsuited for absolute monarchy, he nevertheless announced that nothing was going to change: "I shall maintain the principle of autocracy just as firmly and unflinchingly as it was preserved by my unforgettable dead father." In this attitude he was enthusiastically supported by his young wife; in fact, right from the start, Alix —or Alexandra, as she was now called—felt that Nicholas was inclined to be too unaggressive. Even before they were married, she had written him the first of what were to be many messages urging him to take a stronger stand: "Show

Peasants awaiting their gifts jam a Moscow field at the time of the coronation. Painted for the royal family, the gay water color at left carries no hint of the tragic stampede that followed. At right, in the work of an artist critical of the czarist regime, survivors identify victims and mourn the dead.

The three oppressors of the old regime—priest, czar, and capitalist—appear as colossal statues in the revolutionary poster at left. Signaling their overthrow, a defiant worker puts a torch to the massive figures. The 1880 engraving at right, from an American magazine, depicts an underground meeting of anticzarist conspirators. Alerted to approaching police by a guard at the door, the man standing at center with a gun reaches to extinguish the light so they can escape.

your own mind and don't let others forget who you are."

All that was needed to make the reign of Nicholas II just as undemocratic and reactionary as his father's was government ministers who leaned the same way, and during his early years as czar there was no lack of these. Liberals at the universities, reformers attempting to work at the local level through the *zemstvos*, journalists who tried to advance new social ideas in their newspapers—all were systematically repressed and persecuted, while the police ferreted out revolutionaries of every description. Minority groups, too, such as the Poles, the Finns, and the Jews, were treated with cruel injustice; Nicholas II permitted one of the worst massacres of Jews—at the city of Kishinev in 1903 —before the Nazi atrocities of World War II. It was his naïve belief that "nine tenths" of political agitators and revolutionaries were Jews, whereas in fact nearly all of

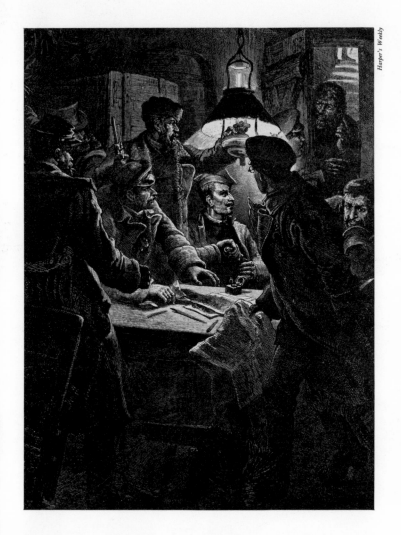

Harper's Weekly

his major critics were Christian, many of them noblemen.

But suppression breeds opposition, and a wide variety of groups opposed to the Russian autocracy continued to meet and talk and think and plan ways of reaching out toward greater freedom. There were two basic groups: the true revolutionaries, who felt that only a more or less violent overthrow of the existing regime could save Russia; and the liberals, who felt that if the Czar would grant certain fundamental reforms, the nation could gradually work its way toward constitutional liberty without bloodshed.

Feeling the need for tighter organization, the revolutionaries formed "parties"—not political parties in the usual sense, since there was as yet no question of elections, but societies whose aim was to bring about a revolution by arousing the people. The largest of these organizations was that of the Socialist Revolutionaries, or SR's, as they were

OVERLEAF: *The Russian peasant, in this 1905 American cartoon, is being attacked by a gigantic octopus labeled Bureaucracy and bedecked in czarist crown and robe. A small axe marked National Assembly—for the parliament reformers sought—is an inadequate weapon against the grasping tentacles of exile, oppressive taxation, graft, religious intolerance, and greed.*

Puck, JUNE 21, 1905

NAT'L ASSEMBLY

EXILE

OPPRESSIVE TAXATION

DESPOTISM

GRAFT

MANN LITH CO PUCK BLDG N.Y.

THE STRUG

THE SLAV.

Karl Marx

Georgi Plekhanov

Lenin, age 22

often called. This party was an outgrowth of The People's Will of the earlier period, and its program called, above everything else, for turning over all land to the peasants who worked it. The power of the czar and indeed the czar himself would be eliminated in a relatively quiet revolution and be replaced by a more enlightened government.

The Social Democrats, or SD's, whose name sounded more peaceful, were actually a much more radical group. These men followed the teachings of the German thinker Karl Marx. In his 1867 book, *Das Kapital*, Marx had predicted a completely new social structure in which all natural resources, and everything else that could be used to produce goods of any kind, would belong to the government in the name of the people. This new system would be called communism. It would come, Marx said, after a total revolution by "the proletariat"—that is, the working class. Under the old system, capitalism, the workers owned little beyond the clothes on their backs, even though their labor produced the world's wealth.

The Social Democrats, or Russian Marxists, were such a clear threat to the existing society that the Czar's police made it impossible for their leaders to stay in Russia. Georgi Plekhanov, the "father" of the movement, set up his headquarters in Switzerland. Young Lenin tried to teach Marxism to the factory workers of St. Petersburg but was sent into exile in Siberia for three years. There he spent his time studying communist theory and writing. When he was released, he settled in Munich, Germany, where he edited a revolutionary newspaper called *Iskra*—"The Spark"— which was smuggled regularly into Russia.

By 1903 it was already clear that Lenin was determined to lead the Russian Marxists the way a general leads an army. Rather short and stocky, with a domelike bald head, he was personally not very impressive until he began to speak. Then the enormous intensity of the man would begin to show: the iron will and the tireless, ambitious drive. Lenin argued constantly and vehemently for the violent overthrow of the czar and the capitalist class, so that a "dictatorship of the proletariat" could be established to pave the way to true communism. "There is no other man who is absorbed by the revolution twenty-four hours a day," a fellow conspirator wrote of Lenin, "who has no other thoughts but the thought of revolution, and who, even when he sleeps, dreams of nothing but the revolution."

Typically, Lenin scorned Social Democrats who wanted to take a more gradual course toward revolution—and his insistence brought about a split in the party. At a series of argumentative meetings, which began in Brussels and ended in London in 1903, Lenin got more than half of his forty-two fellow conspirators to vote for his revolutionary program. From that moment on, the Russian Marxists who followed his lead were known as Bolsheviks, a name adapted from the Russian word for "more." This could be interpreted as *more* members, a majority, or a *more* radical program. The minority at the 1903 meetings, who disagreed with Lenin, were called Mensheviks; and these names were to stick throughout the revolutionary history of the Social Democrats, regardless of which group was in fact larger at any given moment.

In Russia the *real* majority of social reformers were neither SR's nor SD's but rather were moderate liberals who had not yet organized into parties. Most of them had studied British constitutional history, admired the parliamentary system, and hoped that the Czar might allow a similar system to be set up in Russia. They were about to have better luck in that direction than could reasonably have been expected at the turn of the century. In 1904 Nicholas II managed to get his nation embroiled in a war with Japan that would shake his autocracy to its foundations.

Maintaining a tight censorship of the press, czarist police were vigilant in their search for revolutionary propaganda. In a raid on an illegal press, below, police confiscate newspapers and arrest the agitators who printed them.

III   A GREAT

CHANCE MISSED

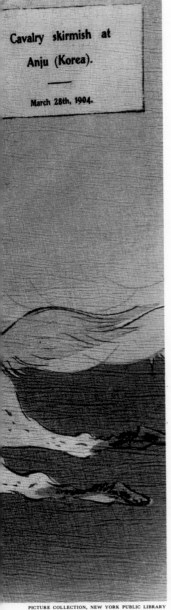

Cavalry skirmish at
Anju (Korea).

—

March 28th, 1904.

One day early in his reign, Nicholas II was riding in his royal carriage with Kaiser Wilhelm of Germany. Sixteen years later these two monarchs were to face each other in a long and devastating war, but now they were on polite if not friendly terms. Wilhelm, a first cousin of Alexandra's, was also distantly related to Nicholas. The Kaiser, who had ambitions to expand Germany's overseas holdings, asked the Czar if he would object to a German seizure of the Chinese port of Kiaochow. Nicholas said he would not mind, and afterward he justified his agreement to one of his ministers on the ground that the Kaiser was his guest and he did not wish to be discourteous to him. When Germany did indeed take over Kiaochow, Nicholas made a step in the same direction by obtaining a "lease" of Port Arthur, another strategic port on China's Yellow Sea.

When governments are in trouble at home, it is often thought to be a good device to distract the people by getting involved in some international adventure. In 1904 this was what Nicholas was persuaded to do by his reactionary ministers, who thought that "a small victorious war" would cure some of the great discontent that was disturbing Russia —perhaps it might even stave off a revolution.

Korea looked like a good place to start trouble, and Russia made a gesture toward occupying that country—much to the anger of the Japanese, who had the same idea. The result was a relatively "small" but far from "victorious" war with Japan, for right from the start the Japanese army and navy got the jump on the Russians. They landed troops in Korea and blockaded Port Arthur. Then Japanese divisions moved into Manchuria to drive back the troops the Czar had sent to the Pacific on the Trans-Siberian Railroad.

Russia's attempt to gain control of Korea was blocked by Japan in the war of 1904–05. A Japanese artist depicted a countryman unhorsing a Cossack in a cavalry skirmish at Anju, 80 miles south of the Manchurian border.

Nicholas II (left) enjoys a carriage ride with Kaiser Wilhelm II of Germany during one of the frequent visits the two distant cousins paid one another in the years before they became World War I enemies. Nine years older than Nicky (as Cousin Willy familiarly addressed the Czar), the Kaiser insisted that they exchange uniforms and once even hinted he wanted Nicky's yacht as a gift.

Over several months, Russia suffered heavy losses. Instead of distracting the Russian people, the unsuccessful war made them angrier with their government. In January, 1905, Port Arthur fell to the Japanese; in May a Russian fleet of antiquated warships, which had laboriously steamed twelve thousand miles to do battle with the Japanese navy, was almost entirely destroyed in the Sea of Japan.

Meanwhile, in the late fall of 1904, a convention of representatives from the *zemstvos* had respectfully but unanimously asked the Czar for national reforms. First they requested a guarantee of such civil liberties as freedom of the press, freedom from arbitrary arrest, and freedom of assembly. They also asked for a representative body—a kind of parliament or congress—to act with the Czar in either a consultative or legislative capacity. This request was enthusiastically supported by a large number of professional societies, such as those of the lawyers, the doctors, the engineers, and the journalists. It became clear that the better-educated classes of Russians were going to insist on moving the country toward democracy.

One group in the national movement of protest was composed of the factory workers—Lenin's "proletariat"—who now made up a considerable part of the working population, especially in and around St. Petersburg. The police had been well aware that the Social Democrats were energetically propagandizing this important group, and they invented a peculiar way of countering the Marxist influence. Secretly they enlisted a priest known as Father Gapon, whose job was to pretend to lead the workers in a "socialist" organization. This, the police hoped, would serve to let off

Jolly and confident, Russian sailors crowd the decks of a warship. Without making advance preparations for refueling en route or seeing that all ships were seaworthy, the Baltic Fleet set sail in October, 1904, for the seven-month voyage around Europe and Africa to the Orient. So confused were its commanders that they fired on English fishing boats, mistaking them for Japanese torpedo boats.

注　曙　海
艦　艦

全運送艦
露　国　送　隊　ス
武揚丸　仁川
報国丸　武州丸
天津丸
全武器　船　レトウイザン

Japan launched her war against Russia in February, 1904, with the naval at-
tack on Port Arthur depicted above by a Japanese artist. Guns from Japanese
destroyers churn the water under the silent cannon (right) of Russia's Man-

churian base. Of the two Russian warships engaged, one was sunk and the other escaped, although damage to Russian morale was great. Following this defeat, Russia sent its Baltic Fleet on the ill-fated mission to the Orient.

51

steam and at the same time keep them in close touch with the real revolutionary activities of the proletariat.

Father Gapon, however, was more genuinely concerned with the workers' welfare than the police realized. To dramatize demands for better working conditions and also to support the movement for civil liberties, he decided to have his workers stage a giant "march" on the Winter Palace in St. Petersburg on Sunday, January 22, 1905. There was to be no violence: the workers would simply carry religious banners, sing patriotic songs, and show the government their unanimous desire for a more liberal society.

The crowds—some 200,000 strong—moved slowly and peacefully toward the palace on that winter Sunday morning, but the Czar's guards and the police grew uneasy, and with little warning they began to shoot. Father Gapon was one of the first to fall; about 200 demonstrators were wounded, and 150 were killed.

When news of this massacre spread across Russia, it raised an enormous outcry. Factory strikes broke out like a rash; police and government officials were murdered in scores of towns and villages.

Nicholas quite failed to realize that he had touched off a national revolution. A group of workers were brought to the palace to ask his forgiveness for the demonstration on "Bloody Sunday," as January 22 soon was called. He lectured them on their foolish behavior and warned them against such actions in the future. The SR terrorist organization responded to that by assassinating the Czar's uncle, the Grand Duke Sergius. Nicholas denounced this act in a manifesto urging all loyal Russians to support the autocracy.

But then the Czar made one of those sudden switches that were a clue to his weak and wavering personality. Under pressure from some of his advisors he offered the nation what until that moment Russian reformers had only dreamed of: a representative national assembly, to be known as the Imperial Duma. ("Duma" is derived from the Russian word meaning "to think"; used as a noun, it suggests, like the English word "council," a body of men who would consider and advise on important governmental problems.)

All over Russia there was tremendous excitement at this development, and various groups began to form political parties to get ready for the expected elections and to suggest to the government what the functions of the Duma ought to be. In July, 1905, a congress of representatives from the

Wearing a cassock and cross denoting his religious office, Father Gapon stands thoughtfully amidst a group of his followers. At his left is a nervous police officer.

Rifles raised, czarist forces in a double line face Father Gapon's marchers across a snow-encrusted plaza on Bloody Sunday. A volley seems to have dispersed the group.

zemstvos and town councils issued a statement expressing the fervent hope of the Russian people that "a new order of things" could at last be achieved, and "without convulsions, without bloodshed, without thousands of unnecessary victims."

But when the government announced its precise plans for the Duma in August, there was deep disappointment. The electorate was mainly limited to the nobility, urban bourgeoisie, landed gentry, and peasants acting through the *zemstvos*. Important sections of the populace, including workers and minorities, such as Jews, were excluded. Instead of being a true legislature that could make binding laws, the new body would be just advisory. The Czar and his ministers could take the Duma's advice or leave it.

What followed was one of the most astonishing strikes in modern times. Far from being limited to one industry,

it spread spontaneously from the railroads to every type of factory; from there to power plants, stores, banks, restaurants, newspapers, hospitals—everything shut down as if someone had pulled a gigantic lever. The Russian Empire was paralyzed. In St. Petersburg, in Moscow, in all the big cities, excited crowds roamed the streets waving red flags and listening to street-corner orators demanding democracy for Russia.

This was a showdown, and the Czar's ministers knew it. Count Witte, his leading advisor, who had just concluded a peace treaty with Japan in which Russia came off remarkably well, told the Emperor that only two paths were open. Either Russia must be granted a Duma empowered to make genuine laws, or a military dictatorship must be set up to avoid total revolution. The Czar considered making his second cousin, the Grand Duke Nicholas Nikolayevich, military dictator; but that soldier and patriot announced that he would shoot himself unless the Czar allowed a legislative Duma. "It is necessary for the good of Russia," he

An officer is seized as sailors hoist the red flag of rebellion during the June, 1905, mutiny on the battleship Potemkin, *left. Having shelled the Black Sea port of Odessa in support of a strike, the mutineers took their ship to Rumania. Above, workers fire from their makeshift street barricade.*

55

said, "and of all of us." Very grudgingly, the Czar agreed to "this terrible decision," as he called it in a letter to his mother.

Thus Russia became a constitutional monarchy, at least in theory. The Manifesto of October 30, 1905, provided for fundamental civil liberties and promised to expand the electorate. Moreover, the Duma's approval was to be required for all Russian laws. Everywhere there was gratitude and hope. The liberals, feeling that their day had finally come, proceeded openly to organize a party called the Kadets (after the Russian initials, KD, of their official name, Constitutional Democrats). The moderate conservatives also formed a party, the Octobrists, indicating their satisfaction with the October Manifesto. The extreme conservatives were appalled. They reacted by setting off (with police encouragement) a new series of bloody pogroms against the Jews, who were accused of being responsible for the revolutionary flames now beginning to lick at the structure of Russian society.

As for the Socialist Revolutionaries and Social Democrats, they hardly knew what to do. Many doubted Nicholas' sincerity in issuing the Manifesto. Others feared that the great concession made by the government would let the pressure out of the revolutionary movement like air out of a pricked balloon. The SR's had been agitating strenuously among the peasants, and late in 1905, catching the revolutionary spirit of the rest of the country, thousands of peasants rebelled against their landlords, burning down manor houses and expelling their former masters.

The SD's, for their part, refused to accept the October Manifesto, denouncing it in the pages of a new newspaper called *Izvestia* ("News"), the first issue of which came out the very day of the October 17 proclamation. Under the leadership of the Mensheviks—and especially of a dynamic young man named Leon Trotsky—they formed in St. Petersburg a "Soviet," or council of workers' deputies, which became the model for similar groups in other cities. The basis for representation was one deputy for every 1,000 workers.

The St. Petersburg Soviet tried to continue the general strike with demands for an eight-hour workday; but now

An American cartoonist satirized the 1905 reforms: Terrified by spectral figures, including one at top right wearing the liberty cap of the French Revolution, Nicholas II opens his gloomy palace to the light of progress.

56

the mass of the people were not behind them. The leaders of the Soviet were arrested in December, 1905, while a brief outbreak of violence in Moscow was soon put down by government troops.

The revolution of 1905 was petering out. Elections were indeed held for the Duma, and the results put the moderately liberal Kadets into the largest number of seats. Even they were far too liberal for the Czar, however, and from the start Duma and government faced each other like boxers in a ring.

It can reasonably be said that at this moment in history a great opportunity was open to Russia. The country might have evolved gradually toward a system of representative government of a Western European type, with respect for individual rights, rather than retain as it did the state-oriented system favoring autocracy. The *principle* of representative government had been granted. Economically, the nation was beginning to make huge strides, for Russia's natural resources were second to none; she had plenty of manpower; and Western technology was being very successfully applied to her industries. In some ways the fact that she had been backward was a peculiar advantage: for instance, the big-business, mass-production superfactory, which was still a new thing even in the United States, was installed almost from the start in certain Russian industries—metal production was one—without the slow steps of growth that had been necessary elsewhere.

Unhappily, the great opportunity was missed. On one side, the Duma members spent their energies either squabbling among themselves about political differences or making extreme, idealistic demands on the government that obviously would not be granted. On the other side, the Czar and his leading ministers, having quelled the revolution of 1905 by permitting the Duma to come into existence, began right away to curtail its powers and block its attempts to take an active part in the government of the Russian Empire. Anything dealing with foreign policy, foreign loans, or the army and navy was declared outside the Duma's jurisdiction.

Limited to domestic and civil affairs, the Duma then proposed to the government a new distribution of land to the peasants; Nicholas sent I. L. Goremykin, his aged prime minister, to scold the Duma for this "inadmissible" suggestion; the Duma then passed a resolution censuring the government—that is, the Czar's Council of Ministers. Nicholas was furious, and on July 21, 1906, he dissolved the Duma

A glittering pageant held in St. Petersburg's Winter Palace marked the formal opening of the First Duma on May 10, 1906. In this photograph of the historic moment, Nicholas and Alexandra appear at center behind two church dignitaries leading them toward the ceremonial table at right foreground. Above, candlelight flickers over an impressive array of uniforms and robes.

by imperial decree. The council for which such hopes were held had been in session for only a little over two months.

At this, some 200 liberals in the Duma rushed across the border into nearby Finland, where they actually met under the trees in a forest, and issued a statement urging resistance to the Czar's government. The only important result was that they were blacklisted, so that when a new Duma was elected in March, 1907, the rebels were ineligible. Consequently, the Second Duma had fewer distin-

guished liberals among its membership and was a more conservative group.

In the meantime a new prime minister, P. A. Stolypin, had taken advantage of the temporary absence of the Duma to try to calm the unsettled condition of the country in two rather contradictory ways. With his right hand, so to speak, he had the SR and SD terrorists tried by military courts and shot in large numbers; with his left he rapidly pushed through reform measures that gave the Russian

Members of the dissolved Duma— a few wearing jaunty straw boaters—hold their famous rump session in a Finland forest some 80 miles distant from St. Petersburg.

ROMANOV PLEASURES

Following a custom begun by Alexander III in 1884, Nicholas each year gave his wife an Imperial Easter Egg created by Carl Fabergé, a St. Petersburg jeweler. In 1911 the Czar presented his beloved Alexandra with the egg at left, commemorating the fifteenth anniversary of their coronation. (A hymn of praise to the new Czar had adorned the menu, right, for Russia's last coronation dinner—a repast featuring borsch, young sturgeon, lamb, capons, asparagus, salad, pastries, and fruit in wine.) The gorgeous 1911 *objet de luxe*, just five inches high, is a shell of enameled miniatures depicting the Czar and Czarina and scenes of royal life—all embellished with emeralds and rose-colored diamonds. The 1916 egg, the last to reach the Czarina, was a shell of blackened steel with Alexandra's initials in gold, mounted on shrapnel.

Finding the burdens of politics and war oppressive, Nicholas devoted himself to his family. Above, amidst flowers and peaceful, palatial surroundings, the Romanov children entertain young guests from a military academy one pleasant summer afternoon before their delightfully carefree life was ended.

peasants more personal liberty than they had ever had before. For example, after the emancipation of the serfs, the land each peasant family was entitled to work for its own needs was merely a number of narrow strips among many, all belonging to the village in common—the so-called commune system. Stolypin's new law gave the head of a peasant family individual property rights for the first time, even though the process of bringing the law into effect proved to be painfully slow.

From the shelter of the Imperial Palace at Tsarskoe Selo, Nicholas and Alexandra watched the operation of the First and Second Dumas with dismay. Both of them felt that the very idea of a representative assembly violated the sacred heritage of the Russian autocracy; and as soon as Nicholas found an excuse, he dissolved the Second Duma just as eagerly as he had the First. This time the excuse was a charge that the SD members of the Duma were involved in a plot to get the army to mutiny. The "plot" turned out later to be a police fake, but it was a good enough reason for the Czar, and he sent the Second Duma to their homes after a session that had lasted about three months.

Although the people of Russia had profited very little so far from their evolving parliamentary system, they were by no means willing to give it up, and the Czar's ministers realized that. The revolutionary excitement of 1905 had been replaced by a sullen discontent that expressed itself in various subtle but still unmistakable ways. The most popular Russian song right after the dissolution of the Second Duma, for instance, was written by Maxim Gorky, the famous revolutionary novelist and playwright: it was called "At the Bottom."

So, in 1907, a third Duma was elected—only under a new electoral law rigged in such a way that most members would be heavily biased in favor of the wealthy, conservative class, the strongest supporters of the Russian autocracy. Nevertheless, a majority of the newly elected representatives were intelligent, well-educated men who saw that if Russia was to avoid a disastrous revolution, the process of reform must not be cut off completely. Even this Duma, therefore, seemed hardly likely to please Nicholas and Alexandra, who nervously felt that they had created a monster that would destroy them if it was not kept in a tightly locked cage.

Their fears were somewhat reduced by the fact that in Stolypin they had a very able and hard-working prime

*rime minister for five years,
*olypin clashed often with the
*uma, although he was gaining a
*putation as a reformer at the
me of his 1911 assassination.

minister; and his efforts were matched in the Duma by those of Alexander Guchkov, a colorful soldier of fortune who had traveled widely and fought against England in the Boer War in South Africa. Guchkov was the chief of the Octobrists, the moderate conservatives who now dominated the Duma despite the rigging of the electoral law; and he and Stolypin led the nation to some important accomplishments. Several millions of peasants were able to exchange the separated strips of land allotted to them by the village commune for single farms that truly belonged to them. Individual enterprise came into play, and farm production began to rise sharply.

Manufacturing and railroad building, too, made progress at a good pace, so that one of the closest observers of the Russian scene, the British scholar Sir Bernard Pares, remarks: "There can be no doubt that economically the seven years from 1907 to 1914 were, so far, the most prosperous period in Russian history." Besides great economic advances, the public school system was being greatly expanded during these years, and the army and navy were being overhauled. It can be seen that even though sovereign and Duma had failed to make the most of the chance offered by the revolution of 1905, the colossal and backward Russian nation was finally beginning to move forward at an encouraging rate.

But the hopeful season was due for some very bad weather. Stolypin, who made many enemies because of his brusque and forthright approach to governmental problems, was fatally wounded during a theatrical performance in September, 1911. The Czar, who was also in the audience, wrote his mother an eyewitness account of the incident including the comment: "People were trying to lynch the assassin. I am sorry to say the police rescued him from the crowd." As for Czarina Alexandra, she was not sorry to see Stolypin go. She was incapable of understanding that his strong leadership had temporarily bolstered the shaky foundation of her husband's throne. The stubborn Czarina firmly warned the next prime minister, Count Kokovtsev, that he must not, like Stolypin, "overshadow his sovereign."

In actuality, after Stolypin's death Nicholas was beginning to fall under the shadow not of his prime minister but of a strange intruder named Rasputin, who had no official position yet wielded much power. As a dark contrast to the progressive influence of the Duma, the controversial figure of Rasputin is worth special attention.

IV

TWO CAREERS: RASPUTIN AND KERENSKY

Although the married life of Nicholas II and Alexandra has often been described as a model of domestic bliss, there was one shadow that hung constantly over their household. After producing four pretty daughters, the Czarina had finally given birth to a male child in 1904. But the joy that greeted the arrival of the boy, who presumably would some day be czar, was soon harshly checked. It was discovered that he had inherited from his mother a disease called hemophilia. This affliction causes uncontrolled bleeding at the slightest cut or bruise and can easily be fatal. The royal family lived in dread that they would lose their golden boy, and the Czarina exhausted herself between keeping long vigils over her son and praying for a miracle that might save him.

This was the situation when Grigori Efimovich, called Rasputin, arrived upon the scene, having been introduced to the Czar and Czarina by a grand duchess who had heard about his acts of faith healing. The year was 1905, and for some years this bearded peasant from Siberia had been wandering around Russia as a *starets*, or "elder"—a kind of vagrant pilgrim and self-appointed "man of God."

The known facts about Rasputin were few, but in his part of Siberia he already had a wide and curious reputation. He came from the village of Pokrovskoe, where he had been born about 1871, the son of a relatively well-to-do peasant. He was christened Grigori Efimovich; "Rasputin" was a nickname—given to him, some said, because of his tireless pursuit of girls, for the word means "dissolute." In a slightly different form, however, it also means "crossroads";

Serene and saintly in his simple black caftan, Rasputin appears opposite as the holy man who brought such joy and hope to the trusting royal pair.

his friends said that was the origin of the name, since Pokrov-skoe did in fact stand at the junction of several roads. At any rate, Rasputin had a dual reputation almost from the beginning. He was the most lecherous young man in town, yet he early showed gifts of "second sight" and prophetic powers, which cast a glow of religious sanctity about him. It was said that he could spot a horse thief in a crowd with a single glance and could predict the weather for farmers months ahead. As he grew older, he would disappear from home for long intervals: some said he was fasting and doing penance at monasteries, others that he had joined a secret group known as the *Khlysts*, who held frenzied rites in torchlit forest glades. There seems to be evidence that both sides of the story were partly true.

It was, of course, as a soothsayer and holy servant of God that Rasputin presented himself at the Imperial Pal-

The straw-hatted children of Nicholas and Alexandra romp on a lawn with their pony. Two older girls, Olga (left) and Tatiana, hold the youngest sister, Anastasia, to a precarious seat, as Maria (right) guards little brother Alexis—not too happy with his sailor dress.

ace in 1905, although he did it in a manner that somewhat startled the Czar and Czarina. He came dressed in his crude country boots and caftan, and from the start he was strangely at ease with the royal couple. He greeted them like old country cousins; in no time at all, it seemed, he was addressing them as "Papa" and "Mama" and kissing them casually whenever they met. Both of them were deeply impressed with Rasputin's piercing, hypnotic eyes and his air of rather mysterious self-assurance, as if he knew some unique secret and was on easy terms with supernatural forces. This man seemed to them to be a wonderful example of the great, inarticulate mass of Russian peasants who were their subjects, yet with whom they somehow had never before managed to establish any means of communication.

"The Czar needed a peasant," said one of Nicholas' head courtiers; and the Czarina needed one too. She knew she was unpopular with the Russian upper classes, but she cherished the romantic notion that the millions of obscure Russian peasants were lovingly loyal to her and to the Czar. Rasputin's supernatural air reinforced Alexandra's idea that he was typical of the people, for she devoutly believed that in their untutored faith the simple people of Russia were more directly in touch with God than the ordained priests of the Orthodox Church.

Rasputin soon showed what he could do for young Alexis, the heir-apparent to the throne. He would sit at the bedside of the Czarevich and in direct, colorful peasant language tell enchanting stories of Siberia. When Alexis had a headache, it needed only Rasputin's hand on his brow to make it go away; or sometimes the prophet just spoke to the boy on the telephone, telling him the headache would disappear—which it promptly did. What was far more important, Rasputin demonstrated on several occasions that he could stop the bleeding when the young prince fell or ran into something during his attempts to play like ordinary children. How this was done was a total mystery to the doctors called in by the Czar, but there seems to be no doubt that it was what now would be called a psychosomatic cure. The boy's faith in Rasputin's power was so strong that once the *starets* had convinced him that the bleeding would stop, it really did stop. It was an example of the mind controlling the body to an abnormal degree.

The effect of all this on the Czarina can easily be imagined. To her it was the miracle she had been praying for, incontestable proof that "our Friend" (as she and Nicholas called Rasputin) had been "sent to us by God."

Pleasantly surprised at the shower of good things that began to descend on him once he became a favorite of the royal family, Rasputin set up a comfortable establishment in St. Petersburg. Soon rumors of high living and low pleasures began to filter back to the palace. It was all just spite, Alexandra believed, the kind of thing true saints had often had to endure. In her letters to the Czar she often referred to Rasputin as "Him," and in some sense she considered him to be divine, a kind of reincarnation of Christ.

By 1912 Rasputin was beginning to be an important political figure. His intimacy with the royal family was now well known, and because of it, many people who wanted favors or information, or who hoped to influence the Czar in his decisions, fawned upon Rasputin. Although he did not seem to be personally greedy—except where good food, good wine, and pretty women were concerned—he accepted gifts readily enough, sometimes immediately giving the money away to poor people without even counting it. In return, he would scribble a note in his bad handwriting—he had very little education—to demand a favor of some official. Usually, all the note said was: "My dear friend, do it—Grigori." Usually, that was enough.

The combination of his growing political power and his notorious sexual habits was to make Rasputin a leading topic of discussion in the Fourth Duma, which was elected in 1912. On the whole, the membership in that Duma was conservative; but conservative or liberal, the spectacle of the bearded peasant living in luxury and enjoying first claim on the attention of the Czar and Czarina was more than most upper-class Russians could stand. Moreover, opponents of the regime found in Rasputin's sinister influence a powerful argument to use against the autocracy. Nasty rumors began circulating about the nature of Rasputin's friendship with the Czarina. These almost certainly unfounded tales intensified the dislike that many members of the nobility felt for "the German," as she was often called. Meanwhile the hierarchy of the Orthodox Church was split between those who denounced Rasputin as a creature of the Devil and those who supported him rather than incur the displeasure of the Czar and the Czarina.

About this time, another important figure began to emerge in Russian national affairs—a man as different from Rasputin as day from night. It was Alexander Kerensky, the Duma member who was to act as the communicating link between the Provisional Government and the Soviet after the March revolution.

Kerensky came from the provincial town of Simbirsk, on the Volga River, where he was born in 1881. His father was the headmaster of the two local high schools, and this led to one of the curiosities of Russian revolutionary history. For Lenin, the Bolshevik leader, was also born in Simbirsk and in his teens was the star pupil in a school headed by Kerensky's father. Lenin was about eleven years older than young Alexander, so they were never in school together; yet to Kerensky it always seemed strange that two boys who had "breathed the same air . . . heard the same peasant songs and played in the same college playground" should have taken such different paths to the Russian Revolution and ended as bitter enemies.

Of the two, Kerensky was by far the more typical of the thousands of young Russian intellectuals who, despite their upper-class background, were forced by conscience to struggle against the autocracy of the czars. When he was eighteen, he left his father's comfortable home and went to St. Petersburg to enroll in the university. Although controlled by the government, universities were nevertheless the most active centers of revolutionary thought. "We became the enemies of the Autocracy," Kerensky wrote later, "almost as soon as we entered. . . ."

Kerensky studied law, and shortly after he was graduated, in 1904, he began thinking of devoting his life to the cause of Russian freedom. This soon got him into trouble. As one of a small group putting out a revolutionary weekly called *The Storm-Finch*, he came to the attention of the czarist police. Just before Christmas in 1905 he was picked up for possession of inflammatory leaflets, and he spent four months in solitary confinement. Like most revolutionaries, he regarded this as a badge of honor, and he put the time to good use working out in his mind how he might best use his talents to further the cause when he got out. Normally, a young lawyer's easiest course was to become a civil servant; but Kerensky did not want to be a cog in the machine of government. Instead, he decided to specialize in defending people charged with political crimes, and he soon proved to be a skillful practitioner of this difficult art.

In 1912 Kerensky was one of three "political lawyers" appointed by members of the outgoing Third Duma to investigate an ugly incident at some gold mines in Siberia. There had been a police massacre just as brutal as that of the 1905 "Bloody Sunday"; about 200 people, including both workers and their wives and children, had been machine-gunned to death. The work of the investigating

Young Alexander Kerensky appears ill at ease in the stiff white collar worn for the early photograph at left. Below, survivors awkwardly line the field on which lie the bodies of striking Siberian gold miners and their families, killed in 1912 by czarist police.

commission brought Kerensky much favorable attention, and that same year he was elected as a member of the Fourth Duma. He was a Socialist Revolutionary, but the socialist parties had been outlawed; thus he entered the Duma as a representative of the Trudoviks, or "Group of Toil," a small labor faction formed for that election.

By 1913, Rasputin and the Duma were thus, figuratively speaking, face to face. On the side of the autocracy, the Czar had allowed his reactionary advisors to push him into an attitude of rigid antagonism toward the Duma; Rasputin and the Czarina urged him to dissolve it altogether, or at least deprive it of all its real powers. On the side of reform stood the Duma, among whose leaders Kerensky was one of the most radical. He was a very eloquent public speaker, and whether in the chambers of the Duma or in smaller gatherings, he always impressed people with the fiery intensity of his conviction that Russia must throw off the chains of autocracy and adopt a more liberal form of government.

The opposition between throne and Duma was heightened when, in 1913, the 300th anniversary of the Romanov dynasty was magnificently celebrated and the importance of the Duma in the ceremonies was deliberately slighted. There was an exciting moment in the great Kazan Cathedral when Rasputin insolently sat himself down in one of the seats that had been set aside for the Duma. M. V. Rodzianko, President of the Duma, grabbed the "man of God" by his tunic and bodily threw him out of the church despite Rasputin's effort to outstare him with his glittering eyes. In Kerensky's opinion, the *starets* was "like a living symbol of the decline of Czarism."

As the year 1914 opened, even the more conservative members of the Duma were continually criticizing the Czar, his Council of Ministers, and Rasputin. The chronic dissatisfaction was reflected in the working class by a great increase in the number of labor strikes. The secret police predicted the outbreak of a mass revolution.

Then, in the summer of 1914, something even bigger broke out: World War I.

V THE EMPIRE STAGGERS

L'Illustration

Bayoneted rifles at the ready, the Czar's legions pass in review during a July, 1914, parade held near St. Petersburg for the visiting President and Premier

World War I was the first great war in which the soldiers of the chief nations involved wore steel helmets, and the "tin hat" became almost a symbol of that war. Russia, however, was an exception: her millions of soldiers went to battle in visored cloth caps, which looked very cocky but gave no protection against bullets or flying pieces of shrapnel.

The Russian soldier's jaunty cap suggests much about Russia's role in the war. In spite of recent strides toward industrialization, Russia was still basically an agricultural country. The huge majority of her troops were peasants who had been drafted from remote farming communities. In weapons, equipment, and transport, her army had been only moderately modernized since the "lessons" of the Russo-Japanese War in 1904–05. The valor of the Russian infantryman was Russia's best weapon; but in the end it

of France. Such impressive displays as this convinced Russia's allies that she would be a formidable opponent of Germany in the war that was about to erupt.

turned out to be no match for Germany's heavy artillery, masses of equipment, and the stubborn, systematic fighting of her steel-helmeted soldiers.

At the start, in the summer of 1914, it looked as if the pressure of the war effort against Germany might overcome the crosscurrents of discontent and disunity that rocked the Russian ship of state. On June 28 the heir to the throne of Austria-Hungary was assassinated in the provincial town of Sarajevo. The plot was traced to the small neighboring country of Serbia, which Russia was pledged to defend. Austria then made demands that threatened Serbia's independence, and Germany stood behind Austria. Thus it was that by the beginning of August, 1914, Russia reluctantly found herself confronting war with both Germany and Austria. She was not alone; but her powerful friends, France and England, were far away.

The Russian people, most of whom heartily disliked everything German, rallied enthusiastically behind the Czar's government. Soon after the declaration of war the name of the imperial capital was changed from the German-sounding St. Petersburg to the more acceptable Russian name, Petrograd. The patriotic excitement—which, incidentally, was duplicated in every other country that went to war, including Germany—seemed to overwhelm nearly everyone. Yet Rasputin, who was in his Siberian village recovering from a stab wound given him by an angry woman, sent an ominous telegram to the imperial palace: "Let Papa [the Czar] not plan war; for with war will come the end of Russia and yourselves, and you will lose to the last man."

In France and England it was hoped that Russia's enormous army would smash into Germany by sheer force of numbers, and people spoke optimistically of "the Russian steam roller." The figure of speech was not a good one, for the Russian army was unable to maintain any momentum. At the front, everything depended on men and horses; there were no tanks and comparatively few airplanes; there were hardly any motor trucks and practically no roads solid enough for them to use anyway. Russian field artillery, though excellent in quality, fired relatively small shells, which always seemed to be in short supply. Bringing up matériel and reinforcements from the rear was a task that fell almost entirely on the Russian railroad system. It soon proved to be hopelessly inadequate.

Nevertheless, with a gallantry that aroused the admiration even of the German generals opposing them, the

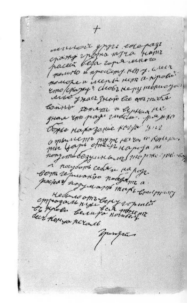

BILD-ARCHIV, ÖST. NATIONALBIBLIOTEK, VIENNA

Austrian soldiers with slung rifles guide a column of Russian war prisoners, many of them in tall fur hats, through a Galician village. As Russia's offensives collapsed, such scenes were often reenacted on the wide Eastern Front.

In the nearly illegible scrawl at left, Rasputin warns the Czar of "calamity, great sorrow, gloom" to come from the war. At top is the cross he used on his letters.

Russians struck hard against Germany and Austria in the summer of 1914. In the north they invaded East Prussia with much success at first, for the Germans at this early stage of the war were concentrating on France. In the south, Russian armies attacked the Austrian province of Galicia with equally good luck. Germany, however, rushed reinforcements to both fronts by means of her excellent railroads, and by the end of 1914 the Russians had been stopped, and in some places, heavily thrown back.

Their losses were appalling. The German artillery dumped thousands of tons of high-explosive shells on the Russian infantry, slaughtering them by whole battalions— sometimes the Czar's soldiers did not even get a glimpse of their enemy. Advancing against German infantry, Russian officers held to the brave but old-fashioned idea that an officer should never crawl—and efficient German machine-gunners mowed down the easy targets. Ammunition supplies became disastrously low: many a Russian regiment attacked without artillery support; with only a few rounds of cartridges for their rifles, the men had to depend on their bayonets. Some of the units even were short of rifles, and soldiers often had to go without until they could pick up the weapons of fallen comrades. The war was proving to be larger, longer, and far more devastating than anyone could have forecast at the outset. Unlike her enemies and allies, Russia was not able to increase production of war goods enough to meet the enormous demands of a prolonged conflict.

Before the war was a year old, prospects for a Russian victory were dim. Nearly *four million* Russian soldiers had been lost: killed, wounded, or taken prisoner. There were not nearly enough doctors or field hospitals, which meant that thousands upon thousands of untended wounded men suffered horribly. "The regular army," wrote a top Russian general, "had vanished." Replacements more often than not were half-trained peasants who barely knew how to fire a rifle—when and if they could get one.

At this critical point, Nicholas decided that what the Russian armies needed was to have their Czar on active duty at the front, leading them in battle for the glory of Mother Russia. It was a foolish notion, for Nicholas had no practical experience as a military commander and only

Dressed in full Cossack uniform, the Czar poses on horseback, surrounded by members of his most famous fighting troops. Such appearances at the front by Russia's ruler-turned-commanding-general were supposed to reinvigorate the nation's badly sagging war effort.

the haziest concepts of military strategy and tactics. But it appealed strongly to his romantic and patriotic nature—and it got him away from the tedious pressure of reports, conferences, and decisions that faced him every day in Petrograd or at Tsarskoe Selo.

The Czar's decision to go a-soldiering could not have been worse for war-torn Russia, and it was vehemently opposed by nearly all his ministers and advisors. But the little emperor who could sometimes be so easily swayed could also be very obstinate about something close to his heart. On September 2, 1915, he presided over a meeting of the Council of Ministers at the Imperial Palace. Almost desperately the ministers argued that his going to the front would amount to a kind of abdication—that is, it would in effect leave the Russian throne vacant at the seat of the government. Nicholas listened with a show of his usual politeness, holding clenched in his hand a religious icon, a small picture of one of the saints. (It probably was the icon, an image of Saint Nicholas, that his wife had given him to take to military headquarters; it had been blessed by Rasputin.) When everyone had finished speaking, he got up and said simply: "I have heard what you say, but I adhere to my decision." A day later he left for the front.

There is no doubt that both Rasputin and the Czarina encouraged the Czar to take command of the armies despite the advice of his ministers. Alexandra was jealous of the Grand Duke Nicholas Nikolayevich, the commander in chief, a man who towered nearly a foot above her husband and who was very popular with the Russian soldiers. This was bad enough, she thought; but in addition, the Grand Duke showed no respect whatever for her favorite holy man. Rasputin had proposed a trip to headquarters so that he could personally hang up an icon there—to which the Grand Duke is reported to have replied by telegraph: "Come and I'll hang."

Rasputin had naturally been affronted by the Grand Duke's snub; yet he realized that with the Czar away at the front for long periods, he would be able to exert his influence over the Czarina even more strongly. The opposition of many members of the Duma, who had become quite outspoken in their attacks on him, could be countered by getting Alexandra to persuade her husband to appoint Rasputin's friends as ministers.

In this way began one of the most astonishing episodes of modern times, whereby a badly informed and superstitious empress sabotaged the government of a great empire

L'Illustration

An imposing six feet six inches tall, the Grand Duke Nicholas is helped by an aide into a fur-lined coat. Equally impressive is the medal display covering his chest.

Each man a perfect target, Russian soldiers cross a field from which trees have been cleared to attack Austrian defenses. Such advances led to heavy casualties.

by constantly nagging the emperor to make the governmental changes recommended by an ignorant Siberian peasant. This would have been crippling at any time, of course, but under the awful strain of the war it was to be calamitous.

As a matter of fact, the Czar's rejection of his ministers' plea that he stay at the helm of the government marked a sharp turning point in Russian history. After this decision

had been made, there could be little chance of stopping the country's plunge toward revolution.

Even while Nicholas was trying to make up his mind whether to take personal command of the armed forces, evidence had been mounting from all sides that the people of Russia were ready for a last tremendous effort to work together as a unified nation under the Czar. But it was necessary first for the Czar to acknowledge the terrible

81

The Duma's wartime attempt to exercise more political power while the Czar was busy with military matters is ridiculed in the German cartoon at left. Baby Nicholas, surrounded by such grim toys as a gallows, a guillotine, and a padlocked prison, looks up in fright at the huge, menacing Duma and exclaims: "How my dolly has changed!"

pressures that the war was bringing to bear upon his country by granting some fundamental reforms. He would have to fulfill the promises of the 1905 revolution.

Already the leading citizens of the country, working through the Duma and through organizations set up by their local governments, had voluntarily taken into their own hands many of the war problems that ought to have been solved by the Czar's government. The *zemstvos* of thirty-five Russian provinces, for instance, had combined with a national council of mayors from the larger cities and formed what was called Zemgor, the Russian Red Cross. Zemgor did much to help the struggling Russian army, providing hospitals, medical supplies, food, transportation for wounded soldiers, and many other essential services.

The critical problem of supplying enough matériel for the army—especially ammunition—also was tackled by a citizens' group, headed by M. V. Rodzianko and Alexander Guchkov. They proposed a national Defense Council for this purpose. The Czar agreed that it should be established, much to the distress of the Czarina, whose comprehension of warfare hardly went beyond her son's toy soldiers, and whose hatred for "that horrid Rodzianko" was constantly growing. "Russia, thank God, is not a constitutional country," she reminded her husband. "[yet] these creatures try to play a part. . . . it is a fright if one gives in. . ." The Defense Council was nevertheless approved by the Duma in August, 1915, and by early 1916 it had begun to increase the flow of supplies to the army.

But although Nicholas was reasonable and cooperative about anything that had to do directly with the welfare of Russia's armed forces, he was strangely insensitive to the deep desire of his people for a better society. Any re-

Raising his cross in blessing, a priest walks among wounded Russian soldiers (below), who are lying on straw in a church hastily converted to a makeshift hospital. Volunteer nurses attend the men in this 1916 picture of the front.

CHARLES PHELPS CUSHING, NEW YORK

83

Two men who tried to bring order to Russia's chaotic war effort: Alexander Guchkov (above), a Red Cross official who later helped organize war industries, and Duma President Rodzianko (below).

form, he believed, would simply have to wait until war's end. "In general I don't pay attention to what they say," he had remarked blandly to his Minister of War when the Duma met at the beginning of August. To a certain extent his going off to army headquarters was an expression of his disdain for dealing with the elected representatives of the people.

Ironically, the Czar's departure not only aroused a joint protest from his Council of Ministers, but it also helped bring the quarrelsome political groups in the Duma into closer agreement than they had ever reached before. With the exception of the Marxists and socialists on the extreme left and the reactionary conservatives on the far right, they combined to form what was known as the Progressive Bloc. Their program, which was widely published, called above all for "a Government based on the confidence of the public," pointing out that "only a strong, firm, and active Government can lead the country to victory." They wanted the Czar to choose a new Council of Ministers who would work in close harmony with the Duma and Zemgor and thus give Russia a government more responsive to the will of the people.

But it was not to be. Hardly had Nicholas reached his headquarters at "the front"—actually, Mogilev was a comfortable place a safe distance behind the lines—when he began to receive a torrent of letters from Alexandra. She wrote every day, pouring out everything pell-mell in her rather offbeat English: details of her health; the children's doings; who had come to tea; the latest words of wisdom from Rasputin; and last, but not least, her conferences with the old Prime Minister, I. L. Goremykin, who came to consult with her often.

It was through this ancient gentleman, who had been Prime Minister back in the days of the First Duma and who had now returned to office, that the Czarina kept track of what was going on in the Fourth Duma and in the Council of Ministers. In her very first letter to Nicholas after he left for headquarters, she showed her intention of keeping her hand, guided by Rasputin, firmly on the government:

Do not fear for what remains behind. . . . Lovy, I am here, don't laugh at silly old wify, but she has 'trousers' on unseen, & I can get the old man [Goremykin] to come & keep him up to be energetic. . . . It is all much deeper than appears to the eye . . . you showing your mastery, proving yourself the Autocrat without wh. Russia cannot exist. . . . God is with you & our Friend for you—all is well. . . . Sleep well my Sunshine, Russia's Saviour. . . .

A 1916 photograph, perhaps taken by a member of the royal family, shows the Czarina sitting on a corner of the Czar's desk, as her husband attends to his paper work. This picture, along with Rasputin's letter on page 76, are from a collection of documents discovered in 1962 in a Paris attic.

And in the same letter she began to badger him to get rid of the Minister of the Interior, whom she despised, and appoint in his place a man named Alexis Hvostov, whose only apparent qualification for the job was that Rasputin was on good terms with him. Before long she was to succeed in winning this appointment; and Hvostov turned out to be typical of most of the men Alexandra and Rasputin managed to put into powerful positions: rotten through and through.

Before that happened, however, Goremykin went to headquarters in mid-September, 1915, to discuss with the Czar the demands of the Progressive Bloc—or rather, since he fully shared the opinions of the Czarina about the Duma, to warn his master of this new surge toward democracy. Nicholas sent him back with authority to suspend the Duma immediately.

Even the more conservative members of the Council of Ministers were indignant when the suspension was announced to them. After Rodzianko informed the Duma

OVERLEAF: *Dressed in peasant garb, his hypnotic eyes staring at the camera, Rasputin is surrounded by admirers—mostly women—in this intimate photograph, originally published in 1917 in a French magazine. It appears that the enraptured ladies have shared a teatime snack with the* starets.

L'Illustration

85

members that they must go back to their homes, it was all he could do to get them peacefully to leave the Duma chamber at the Tauride Palace. Petrograd's big factories staged a two-day strike to show their resentment at the government's having taken a step backward just when everyone else was eager to move ahead. On September 19 Zemgor chose delegates to go to the Czar's headquarters and express its feeling that the Duma must be quickly called together again. Nicholas flatly refused to see the delegation. It was clear that the Czarina's constant demands that he be "more autocratic" were achieving results.

There was a glimmer of renewed hope when the Czar ordered the entire Council of Ministers to report to him at headquarters. Was it possible that he had decided, after all, to reorganize his government along the lines suggested by the Progressive Bloc? Those who hoped so would have been disturbed to know that the meeting had been planned in consultation with the Czarina. She had actually advised Nicholas to prepare for the meeting by combing his hair several times with a comb given him by "our Friend," as a kind of magical protection against "those odious Ministers." Instead of making any concessions, the Czar rebuked them for listening to the "radical" proposals of the Progressive Bloc. Soon afterward he began to replace them by more docile men recommended by Alexandra. The first was Hvostov, as Minister of the Interior—a post in some ways the most powerful in the empire, since it carried with it control over the secret police and censorship of publications.

The consequence of Czarina Alexandra's mismanagement of national affairs—always with Rasputin's advice— was summed up neatly by the former commander in chief of the army, the Grand Duke Nicholas: "It is now a reign of chaos." Chaos is hard to describe, and in order to give briefly some idea of what went on in Russia during the year and a half after the Czar went to the front, it is better to show the typical character of events instead of relating them one by one.

The atmosphere that enveloped Petrograd between the fall of 1915 and the winter of 1916–17, and from there spread like a fog to every corner of the Russian Empire, was one of intrigue, disillusionment, and social collapse.

Since Rasputin was a key figure, enormous amounts of time and money were spent by those in the know in attempts to buy and use his influence with the Czarina. But these attempts at intimacy with him, which included bribing, concealing his sexual exploits from Alexandra, and having him followed everywhere by secret police to "protect" him, were often complicated by intense jealousy of his power. Hvostov, for instance, whom the Czarina had ardently supported as Minister of the Interior, got involved in a plan to have the "man of God" murdered. Although his plan miscarried, its discovery meant his downfall with the astonished and furious Alexandra.

Hvostov was merely one of a fairly rapid succession of ministers, most of whom were either grossly incompetent or corrupt or both. The most outstanding example was the Prime Minister who replaced old Goremykin: a disaster named B. V. Stürmer. This widely hated tool of Rasputin, it was hinted in Duma speeches, was no better than an agent of the German enemy. With the rapid changes of high officials, the Russian government had neither dignity nor stability—"ministerial leap frog," one member of the Duma called it. The last Minister of the Interior before the revolution was perhaps the worst yet: A. D. Protopopov, a weak and foolish man believed by many who knew him to be on the edge of insanity.

The combination of such a shambles in the government and Russia's terrible defeats before the guns of Germany produced in the populace a feeling of deep and cynical disillusionment. Gone was the patriotic fervor of 1914; it was replaced by despair, a feeling of unavoidable defeat. "Getting empty in the villages," a peasant said to a British visitor; and indeed it was, as the millions of killed and maimed were followed by thousands more with every passing week. The agony of these losses was not relieved by the knowledge that the woman now guiding Russia's policies was herself of German birth: many suspected her, unjustly, of secretly sympathizing with the enemy.

One of the worst features of the war as conducted by the Russian government was a terrible lack of coordination between the front and the rear—between what was controlled by the generals and what was controlled by civilian officials. Even the Minister of War had a very limited authority over the army's general staff; he was unable to override some of its most harmful policies.

The generals decided, for instance, that as the Germans relentlessly advanced into Russian territory, they would do what Russian generals had done in 1812, when Napoleon had unsuccessfully invaded Mother Russia. This was the "scorched earth" policy of destroying everything that might be of use to the enemy as the Russian armies retreated: burning crops, deliberately wrecking water supply

Scenes of war's terrible desolation: At left, Russian prisoners are set to work chopping rock for their enemy's roads. Below, Austrian soldiers, their knapsacks bursting with booty, leave a thatched-roof village in flames. At right, Russian refugees with their livestock clog a mud road to the rear.

systems, blowing up bridges. This of course made the invaded areas uninhabitable for the local Russian citizens, and several millions of them were forced to flee eastward with the few possessions they could carry away from their broken homes. The roads were glutted with overloaded peasant carts and milling crowds of terror-stricken refugees, many of them sick and near starvation.

The immense stream of uprooted, desperate, suffering humanity [said a report of a discussion by the Council of Ministers] rolls along the roads interfering with military traffic and completely disorganizing the rear of the army. . . . Men and women die by the hundred from hunger, exposure, and disease. The death rate among the children has reached a terrible height. Unburied corpses are left along the roads. The decaying carcasses of dead animals poison the atmosphere. And this flood of humanity spreads over all Russia, adds to war-time hardships, creates a shortage of foodstuffs, increases the cost of living, and accentuates the discontent which is nowhere lacking. . . .

By the fall of 1916 the food shortage and the high cost of living had become acute problems. Actually, as one of the world's greatest agricultural countries, Russia had plenty of food—the difficulty was in moving it to where it was needed. The peasants who produced the food were not anxious to sell their produce for money that would buy almost nothing, since nearly all manufactured goods were now being consumed by the armed forces. What they did sell, or what was taken by the government, often rotted in freight cars waiting in vain for engines to pull them across Russia's overburdened railroad network.

Meanwhile, prices skyrocketed. By Christmas of 1916, fuel was so scarce and expensive in the cities that only the well-to-do could buy it. The average factory workman found himself paying three and four times as much for food and clothing as he had paid at the start of the war—and even at that, his wife had to stand in long lines for hours every day before she could get into a shop to buy her skimpy share. "The mass of industrial workers are quite ready to let themselves go to the wildest excesses of a hunger riot," said a police report for October, 1916.

Short of riots, the factory workers naturally expressed their frustration by strikes, which increased at an alarming rate. At the end of October a great wave of strikes closed nearly every plant in Petrograd. When soldiers were called out to help the police drive the workers back to the factories, they shot at the police instead of at the strikers. This was an omen of things to come, even though the mutiny was quickly put down by four regiments of mounted Cossacks.

Throughout all this the three individuals most responsible continued blindly on their way. Rasputin, knowing full well that he was surrounded by enemies, jockeyed the Council of Ministers around as best he could for his own safety. And he continued to pass his suggestions to the Czarina, for transmission to the Czar.

Alexandra understood nothing of the abyss toward which the empire was rushing. She never doubted that "our Friend" was inspired by a God who would not let the imperial crown fall from her husband's anointed head, and she incessantly begged Nicholas to do what their holy man desired.

And Nicholas, isolated at military headquarters, bored as much as he was distressed by the hundreds of insoluble problems pressing down upon him, retreated further and further from his responsibility. Sometimes he feebly resisted Alexandra's urgings for a short time, but in the end he nearly always gave in again. He even managed to convince himself that his strong-willed wife would take care of everything: ". . . you do great service to me and to our country," he wrote her in the fall of 1916; "I am so happy to think that you have found at last a worthy occupation!"

Then, on December 30, 1916, the Czarina interrupted her daily letter to the Czar with a startling piece of news: ". . . our Friend has disappeared."

Rasputin had actually been murdered. It was already too late for his removal to make much difference in the course of Russian history, and the facts about the crime are

One of the world's leading producers of food, Russia had a wartime shortage of transport to move produce from the farms to cities crowded with war industry workers. Hardships endured by Petrograd residents are shown in two photographs. At left, a street vendor displays a small catch of fish to passers-by. Below, bundled against the cold, men and women vie for sleds, which were serving in place of wheeled vehicles.

93

A Russian cartoonist depicted Rasputin as a frowning giant with the royal couple balanced on his knees like puppets. The long-nosed Czarina beams at her husband, who casts his simpering grin away from her.

obscure. Nevertheless, the story is worth telling as an illustration of the corrupt and sinister atmosphere in upper-class circles of Petrograd on the eve of the March revolution.

Rasputin was killed on the night of December 29, 1916, by some Russian aristocrats who had lured him to the basement of a Petrograd family mansion, or palace. His body, shot, stabbed, and brutally beaten, was found by the police: it had been bound and dropped into the Neva River. Although the assassins at first loudly denied their guilt, they soon realized that they would be considered heroes for having done away with the *starets*. Moreover, they felt certain that they would not be severely punished, since one of them was a grand duke, another a prince married to a niece of the Czar's, and a third a prominent member of the Imperial Duma. Before long they were boasting about the murder to their friends.

The motive for killing Rasputin is said to have been a patriotic desire to rid Russia of an evil influence. Yet the character of the three chief conspirators (there were five in all) was hardly more admirable than that of their victim. The ringleader was Prince Felix Yusupov, twenty-nine-year-old heir of one of Imperial Russia's wealthiest families. By his own description, he was a spoiled playboy who had spent his youth in gay carousing in Petrograd, Paris, and London. One of his favorite diversions had been to dress as "an elegant woman" and go out to balls and night clubs, where he drew much flattering attention from gallant army officers unaware of the disguise.

Prince Felix Yusupov

The Grand Duke Dmitri Pavlovich, one of Yusupov's closest friends, was a cousin of the Czar and a favorite of the royal family. His behavior during the war years, however, disturbed the Czarina very much. An officer in the horse guards, he either hung around the Czar's military head-quarters, doing nothing in particular, or went on long leaves to Petrograd to join Yusupov in wild parties and visits to gypsy entertainment spots.

The third principal member of the murder ring was V. M. Purishkevich, a far-right-wing Duma member known for his passionate hatred of all liberals, radicals, and Jews. He was one of the organizers of a group of reactionaries known as the Black Hundreds, who worked with the secret police in promoting anti-Jewish riots. Aside from that, Purishkevich was noted for his witty speeches in the Duma, and sometimes, his scandalous clowning.

Having decided, according to Yusupov's later published account, that Rasputin must be assassinated, the conspirators went about it very deliberately. They decided to poison the "man of God," and a doctor friend of Purishkevich's was called into the plot to provide potassium cyanide. Prince Yusupov had cultivated Rasputin's friendship and invited him to a private party at the palatial Yusupov family mansion on Gorokhovaia Street at midnight on December 29.

It has never been clear why Rasputin agreed to go, especially since there had already been several attempts on his life and he knew that most aristocrats hated him. Yusupov (who was still living in 1967) has told different stories at different times, one version being that Rasputin was eager to meet Yusupov's attractive young wife, Irina, the Czar's niece. (Irina was actually in the Crimea in December, 1916, recovering from influenza.) At any rate, the *starets* was ready and waiting at midnight when Yusupov arrived to pick him up in a motor car; he was dressed in his best clothes—a white silk blouse embroidered with cornflowers, velvet breeches, polished boots, and a raspberry-colored cord for a belt. Obviously he expected some extraordinary entertainment.

At the Yusupov palace elaborate preparations had been made. An unused apartment in the basement had been specially furnished as if it were a stage-set for a melodrama: rich draperies and rugs had been installed, heavy tables and carved chairs moved in, lanterns hung, and a cozy fire built in the big granite fireplace. Why it was thought necessary to poison Rasputin in these surroundings rather than in one of the upstairs apartments of the big palace has never been explained.

Yusupov claims—and it must be remembered that the story told by the assassins themselves is all we have to go on—that he took Rasputin into the downstairs hideaway and plied him with cakes and wine. The cakes and the glass from which the *starets* drank were heavily poisoned with potassium cyanide—enough, the doctor had promised, "to kill several men instantly." Rasputin looked somewhat ill, but otherwise nothing happened. Amazed and frightened, Yusupov went upstairs to confer with his fellow conspirators, who had been impatiently waiting for news and whiling away the time by playing phonograph records, and apparently, drinking rather heavily.

Yusupov then went downstairs again, he says, taking with him Dmitri Pavlovich's revolver. When Rasputin was not looking, Yusupov pointed the gun at him and pulled the trigger. Rasputin gave "a wild scream" and fell heavily backward onto a bearskin rug. At the sound of the shot, the other conspirators came tumbling down the stairs, accidentally hitting the light switch and throwing the scene into momentary darkness. When the lights came on again, the doctor examined the body and declared the "man of God" to be thoroughly dead. The assassins all went upstairs, congratulating each other that they had succeeded in ridding Russia of the evil *starets*.

Yusupov says that at this point he felt "a vague misgiving"; then "an irresistible impulse" made him go downstairs once more. To his utter horror, Rasputin's "corpse" had come back to life. It rose from the floor, "foaming at the mouth," and attacked Yusupov: "a ferocious struggle began." "I realized now who Rasputin really was," Yusupov wrote later. "It was the reincarnation of Satan himself who held me in his clutches. . . ."

The fantastic tale ends with the superhuman mystic pursuing Yusupov up the stairs and bursting through a "locked" door into a snowy courtyard. Purishkevich chased him outside and felled him again with four shots from a pistol. The amateur assassins finished their job by taking Rasputin's body to a lonely bridge on the Neva River and dropping it over the side, where it broke through the ice. It was later reported that water was found in the lungs of the body, suggesting that Rasputin was still alive when he sank into the Neva.

During all these macabre goings-on the police had not been entirely unaware of something amiss at the Yusupov palace, and although they did not find the body for two days, they began an immediate investigation. The Czarina, not surprisingly, was horrified at the disappearance of "our Friend," and she had a definite idea of who the chief culprits were. On December 31, 1916, she telegraphed the Czar at his military headquarters: "I fear that these two wretched boys [Yusupov and the Grand Duke Dmitri] have committed a frightful crime. . . .Start today, I need you terribly."

Rasputin had prophesied that his death would bring doom to the royal family: "So long as I live, the imperial family will also live; when I die, they will also perish." It was to be a year and a half before that prophecy was fulfilled. But there can be no doubt that the murder of the notorious *starets* added to Russia's unsettled state at the end of 1916. The attitude of most peasants, for instance, probably was well expressed by a soldier who said to a government official: "Yes, only one muzhik [peasant] ever got through to the Czar, and him the masters killed."

As for the Czar and the Czarina, they did not change their ways after Rasputin's death. As if in vengeance, they went ahead with more bad appointments of stupid and ignorant ministers. The explosive resentment of the Russian people—a resentment now shared by a very broad cross section that included many members of the nobility as well as peasants, soldiers, and workers—could not be contained much longer. The year 1917 opened with many rumors of plots on the part of highly placed aristocrats to assassinate the Czar.

None of the plots of the distraught nobility came to anything: they were too disorganized to act. But the long-suffering common people, without quite realizing it themselves, were about to act. Their act was to go down in history as the March Revolution.

VI TOWARD A SECOND REVOLUTION

The unexpected insurrection of March, 1917, ended with the national power of Russia in the hands of two rather antagonistic groups. The Executive Committee of the Soviet of Workers' and Soldiers' Deputies was dominated by socialists, with a minority of Bolsheviks. The Provisional Government represented the moderates—some liberal and some conservative—of the old Duma. One man was a member of both bodies. Alexander Kerensky, Minister of Justice in the Provisional Government and Vice-Chairman of the Petrograd Soviet, had the hard task of maintaining a link between the two groups and preventing them from working at cross-purposes.

Revolutionary soldiers pile onto a crowded truck at a snow-covered street corner in Petrograd during the March, 1917, uprising that led to the overthrow of the Czar.

A compromise choice to head the Provisional Government was Prince Georgi Lvov, the able, respected chief of the Council of Zemstvos, Russia's local governing bodies.

Actually, for a while it looked as if all might go well. The Soviet Executive Committee decided that it was best to let the Provisional Government take the lead, while it stood by as a kind of watchdog of the Revolution. This fitted in with left-wing political theory, which assumed that a bourgeois, democratic republic would be necessary as a transition between czarism and socialism or communism.

There was a basic flaw in this assumption—one that both the Soviet's radical socialist leaders and the moderate liberals of the Provisional Government like Kerensky failed to see at first. A democratic republic could function only with the support of broad masses of the people. The public would have to understand the sometimes slow and careful methods by which a representative democracy solves its problems. They would have to understand that liberty implies tolerance for many differing views.

The Russian people sadly lacked experience with democracy. Moreover, the enormous impact of the war, which had hastened the collapse of the outworn system of the autocracy, had left the country in a state of painful disorganization and discontent. The great masses of ordinary Russian citizens were in no mood for delay, especially in solutions to the two problems that seemed to plague their very existence: the continuation of the war and the failure to get more land into the hands of the peasant farmers. They thought these matters should be taken care of quickly, and they felt more and more that if the Revolution meant anything, it meant just that.

The Provisional Government, unfortunately, took a different view. The attitude of Kerensky was typical. Looking as he did toward the Western European democracies as models for the government he hoped to see in Russia, he felt that Russia's military obligations to England and France were binding. Russia must fight on against Germany—despite her appalling losses, despite the desperate state of her economy, despite the plunging morale of her troops. As for the redistribution of land to the peasants, Kerensky felt that it must wait until a Constituent Assembly, scheduled for the fall of 1917, could meet and set up a democratic system for deciding such matters.

Meanwhile, in the first happy flush of the new revolutionary era, the Provisional Government tried to introduce all at once a set of fundamental liberties such as Russian reformers had dreamed of for generations. There was to be freedom of speech and of the press; legal equality for everyone; voting privileges for everyone; complete freedom of

A dynamic visionary of thirty-six, Alexander Kerensky easily overshadowed his older, more conservative colleagues in the Provisional Government. Wearing the uniform he adopted as Minister of War, he studies battle plans.

political activity. In keeping with these reforms, men who had been jailed or exiled to Siberia for political reasons were immediately released; those who were in foreign countries for their own safety were allowed to return.

The new freedom was especially meaningful to the Bolsheviks, who had been forced to operate mostly under cover until the fall of czarism. Now the Bolshevik leaders began to come back to Petrograd like homing pigeons suddenly let out of their cages.

The supreme Bolshevik leader, however, found it impossible to fly straight home. In Switzerland, Lenin had been watching the revolutionary developments in Russia with surprise and pleasure. But Germany, with whom Russia of course was still at war, stood between him and his native land. How could he get back to Russia?

He got there, as it turned out, with the help of the German government. The Germans knew that Lenin would be no more inclined to support the Provisional Government, largely made up of capitalist liberals, than he had been to support the Czar. They also knew that one of Lenin's Ten Commandments of Bolshevism, so to speak, was that the Russian people had no reason for fighting Germany and ought to pull their nation out of the war as soon as possible. During 1916 Germany had suffered huge losses against the Allies on the Western Front, and by early 1917 it was apparent that the United States would soon declare war against her and send millions of troops "over there." A separate peace with Russia was something the Kaiser hoped for very much; with the Eastern Front eliminated, he still might be able to win the war.

Toward the middle of April, 1917, a train carrying about thirty Russian exiles, with Lenin at their head, made its way through Germany to the Baltic Sea. German military authorities allowed its transit only on condition that none of its passengers be allowed out to spread their infectious revolutionary theories in Germany. When the sealed train reached the Baltic, the travelers were hastily embarked for Sweden, and from there they crossed through Finland into Russia. It was the first time Lenin had come home in ten years.

The Bolshevik chief got what can only be called a mixed reception. Members of the Provisional Government knew he was the prince of troublemakers and hostile to their attempts to build Russia into a constitutional democracy, but they knew also that his return with the help of the enemy—that is, Germany—would bring charges of treason

Lenin's return from Switzerland is dramatized in a painting showing him actually at the controls of a locomotive bound for Russia.

Soldiers returned from the front have taken over the former meeting hall of the Duma at the Tauride Palace in this 1917 photograph. The soviets, assemblies of workers' and soldiers' delegates, came to dominate political life.

against him. They decided to leave him alone, hoping that the Mensheviks and Socialist Revolutionaries, who outvoted the Bolsheviks in the Soviet Executive Committee, would keep him subdued.

The Soviet leaders, however, did not quite know how to treat Lenin. He was acknowledged to be one of the great chiefs among socialist politicians, yet it seemed that he had gotten out of touch with reality during his long exile from Russia. They had entered into a working agreement with the Provisional Government, including a policy of limited support to the war effort; but Lenin had given no hint that he was ready to make practical compromises. Just the same, some official notice had to be taken of his arrival, and Nikolai S. Chkheidze, the Menshevik chairman of the Petrograd Soviet, went to the city's Finland Station on April 16 to greet him.

At the station the Bolsheviks, with the cooperation of several contingents of soldiers, sailors, and workers who were sympathetic to them, had arranged a colorful welcome. Banners with revolutionary slogans were hanging everywhere; red and gold triumphal arches had been set up; a military band blared out the Marseillaise and other appropriate tunes. The train was late, and the excitement of the crowd grew. When the returning hero finally arrived and walked into the station, Chkheidze made a short and rather embarrassing speech in which he welcomed Lenin but expressed the hope that he would not work toward any disunity that would injure the Revolution.

Lenin paid no attention to Chkheidze. Instead he greeted the workers, soldiers, and sailors as "Dear comrades" and as "the advance guard of the international proletarian army," winding up with: "Long live the world-wide socialist revolution!" That brought a great cheer from the crowd, and outside the station Lenin was enthusiastically hoisted to the hood of an armored car, where he made another speech denouncing war. Then, with dusk falling and the vehicle's headlights cutting through Petrograd's evening gloom, the welcoming procession began to move slowly across the city. Every now and then it would stop long enough for Lenin to clamber to the top of the armored car and make his speech over again to the people who surged around the street intersections, cheering and singing. Even though the whole affair had undoubtedly been planned carefully by the Bolsheviks, it was impressive to everyone who saw it.

What the Bolsheviks had not planned at all was the way Lenin spoke to them when he attended a reception given by the party leaders that evening. It was as if a football team who imagined that they were doing pretty well in a big game were given a half-time tongue lashing by a coach who told them that, on the contrary, they were about to lose the game. Lenin denounced the Soviet Executive Committee for compromising with the Provisional Government. He insisted that overthrow of the "bourgeois" government could be the only possible goal for the Bolsheviks. Then Russia could make a separate peace with Germany—never mind the Allies!—and begin building a communist society.

"We don't need any parliamentary republic!" he shouted. "We don't need any bourgeois democracy! We

Lenin, a youthful Stalin directly behind him, incites a mob of armed soldiers, sailors, and peasants to revolutionary action. V. Serov's painting is in the stern socialist realism style long favored by Russian Communists.

don't need any government except the Soviet of workers', soldiers', and farmhands' deputies!''

The stunned Bolshevik leaders soon found that Lenin meant exactly what he said. His program of militant revolution, the so-called April theses, was published in the pages of the Bolshevik newspaper, *Pravda*—one of whose chief editors at this time was Stalin.

Despite opposition even from members of his own party, Lenin had history on his side to a great extent in the spring of 1917. Under the guidance of Prince Georgi E. Lvov, the Provisional Government's Prime Minister, the measures taken to meet actual conditions were not very effective. The cost of living continued to mount steadily, and the factory workers grumbled bitterly about that; no vigorous steps were taken to help the peasants toward their hearts' desire, more land; the war dragged on with no prospect of an early peace. In May Professor P. N. Milyukov, the Kadet leader serving as Foreign Minister in the Provisional Government, assured the Allies that Russia would go on fighting Germany till the bitter end. Mass demonstrations protesting Milyukov's pledge broke out in the streets of the capital, and large-scale bloodshed was avoided only with difficulty.

Things did not go much better even after Milyukov resigned, which he did shortly. Guchkov, the former Octobrist who was Prince Lvov's Minister of War, resigned at about the same time. After heated debate the Soviet Executive Committee decided to participate in a "coalition" with the Provisional Government. Five more socialists joined Kerensky, who became Minister of War, in the reorganized cabinet. The Bolsheviks remained aloof, heeding Lenin's slogan: "All power to the Soviets; no support to the Provisional Government." At the First All-Russian Congress of Soviets, held at Petrograd in mid-June, a moderate socialist complained that there was no party in Russia ready to take power. "Yes, there is," shouted Lenin from his seat.

Kerensky, meanwhile, announced his intention of pushing the war against Germany with renewed vigor. Morale in the army had never been lower, as proved by mass desertions, and in some episodes, flat refusals to fight. Yet Kerensky recommended a new offensive against the Austrian sector of the enemy line. The entry of the United States into World War I had encouraged nearly all political elements in the hope that this powerful new ally would somehow enable Russia to defeat Germany. The new Minister of War toured the front, making eloquent speeches to arouse the soldiers. His offensive began early in July and

L'Illustration

soon turned into a serious retreat—not for the Austrians and the Germans who helped them, but for the Russians.

Passionate antiwar feelings erupted into new disturbances in Petrograd when the extent of the losses in Kerensky's offensive were published. It is not quite clear even today whether those riotous events—which became known as the July Days—were actually planned by the Bolshevik headquarters or just quietly encouraged by them. At any rate, the whole thing backfired, from their point of view. Gangs of soldiers and sailors roamed the streets, shooting more or less haphazardly at ordinary citizens and killing or wounding some four hundred. The government called in troops from outside the capital to put down these disorders, and after a few days of terror the city quieted down. The moderate Kadets left the Government, Prince Lvov resigned, and Kerensky became Prime Minister.

Kerensky, standing in the back of an open touring car, salutes parading troops during a visit to the front as Minister of War. Below, the disastrous result of the offensive he launched in July, 1917: terror-stricken Russians, having dropped their weapons at word of a German cavalry attack, flee past a village church toward the rear.

Bodies of the fallen sprawl across trolley tracks at a Petrograd intersection, as an outburst of revolutionary violence sends citizens scrambling for safety. Between the March, 1917, overthrow of czarism and the Bolshevik take-over the following November, a number of disturbances rocked the capital; the most serious unrest was that of the so-called July Days.

Whether the Bolsheviks had really been responsible for the July Days or not, it was widely reported that they had been. The Provisional Government, by now disillusioned with the idea of complete political freedom, attacked the Bolsheviks fiercely, accusing them of being pro-German. *Pravda* was shut down, and orders were issued for the arrest of Lenin and his chief lieutenants, Lev Borisovich Kamenev and Grigori E. Zinoviev. Only Kamenev was caught, however: Lenin and Zinoviev quickly went into hiding, and in September they escaped across the border into Finland. From then until October 22 the Bolshevik chief had to command the operations of his party by long-distance communication—mostly by letters sent to subordinates, such as Stalin, who were still free in Petrograd even though under close observation by the government.

More important than Stalin, at this stage, was the Menshevik leader Leon Trotsky, who had come back to Russia from the United States in May and was ready to join forces with Lenin's Bolsheviks for an overthrow of the middle-class government whenever the time should appear ripe. Claiming to be just as subversive as Lenin, Trotsky arrogantly demanded that the Provisional Government arrest him, too. When he was released in mid-September, he helped the Bolsheviks win a majority vote in the Petrograd Soviet and soon was elected president of that body.

By late summer of 1917 the over-all situation in Russia was as chaotic as it had been a year earlier, when the Czar still ruled. There were endless official and unofficial discussions about what ought to be done: meetings, conferences, congresses, some called by the government, some by the Soviet, some by the various political parties. The most impressive gathering, the Moscow State Congress of late August, brought together 2,400 delegates from all the country's "live forces"—former Duma members, trade unionists, bankers, municipal representatives, and members of various soviets. The Congress soon split into irreconcilable right and left wings—with Kerensky at the center, unable to achieve unity.

The millions of words earnestly spoken in Russia that summer did little to change the realities of the war, the collapsing economy of the country, and the dark mood of most of the soldiers, workers, and peasants. In the provinces, bands of furious peasants drove landlords from their estates and burned their manor houses. In the army thousands mutinied, while thousands more deserted. Without the slightest understanding of the works of Karl Marx, the great masses of the Russian people were gradually drifting into a state of mind that was susceptible to the Bolshevik program of total overthrow of the existing system. Things could hardly get much worse, thought millions of people: why not junk things as they were, and start from scratch—especially if it meant the end of the hated war.

On the other hand, there were those who thought that Russia's real troubles had started when the monarchy fell. Some looked back wistfully to Nicholas II, who was now in exile with his family at Tobolsk, Siberia; others felt that although the days of czarism were gone forever, a right-wing, conservative government might restore some of the old glory.

One of those with strong conservative views was General L. G. Kornilov, whom Kerensky had made commander in chief of Russia's armies. Kornilov demanded suppression of the Bolsheviks and other radical elements and hinted that if the Provisional Government could not accomplish this goal, he would. Rumors of a military *coup*

Two Bolsheviks are being interrogated about their political activities, which were suppressed by the Provisional Government following the July Days. Reaching for his pistol, the officer at right seems ready to end the interview.

In Vladimirov's eyewitness water color above, a family consisting of three women and a boy pull a cart bearing all their worldly belongings across a grim Petrograd square. Caught in the crosscurrents of war and revolution, many residents left the troubled city.

d'état reached Petrograd, and Kerensky promptly dismissed Kornilov. The commander in chief replied by ordering a picked force under General A. M. Krymov to move toward Petrograd.

Kerensky, for all his brilliance, was now on the horns of a dilemma that was too difficult for him. He knew that the mood of the people in general was moving further and further to the left—that is, toward the program that Lenin and his Bolshevik followers kept declaring could be won only by the violent overthrow of the Provisional Government. But to allow Kornilov and his *right-wing* followers to overthrow the government instead would mean a counterrevolutionary reaction that might even restore the monarchy and bring the ex-Czar back from Siberia. Although he remained unsympathetic toward the Marxists, Kerensky was even less sympathetic toward the reactionaries. In desperation he turned to the Soviet.

The Soviet leaders, including SR's and Mensheviks as well as Bolsheviks, immediately took vigorous steps to upset

111

General L. G. Kornilov

Kornilov's counterrevolutionary plans. The Petrograd garrison got ready to fight; the factory workers were issued rifles; barricades were built across the main avenues leading into the city. Several thousand army officers in Petrograd who were suspected of being sympathetic to the Kornilov plan were suddenly arrested. But all this proved unnecessary, for the Soviet's almost total control over the railroad system was an even more powerful weapon. The troops dispatched by Kornilov under General Krymov found themselves derailed onto sidings or left standing in their cars while the locomotives pulling them were detached and taken elsewhere. Soviet leaders then dissuaded the soldiers from marching into the city and firing upon their "brothers." It all ended with the arrest of Kornilov, while General Krymov, who felt that he had been disgraced, shot himself.

The most important result of the Kornilov fiasco was that it gave the Bolsheviks a chance to come out of hiding under the banner of "stop the counterrevolution." Lenin still remained cautiously in Finland, but Trotsky was on the scene in Petrograd, diligently working for the proletarian uprising that both of the Bolshevik leaders were now convinced was inevitable in the near future—inevitable, that is, if they played their cards right.

They did play them right. On October 23 a resolution calling for a definite insurrection was adopted at a Bolshevik meeting. Lenin was present at the meeting, having secretly returned from Finland the day before, his beard shaved off and an odd-looking wig on his bald head to further the disguise. Three days later the Petrograd Soviet set up a Military Revolutionary Committee, supposedly to organize the defenses of the capital against possible German attack. Dominated by the Bolsheviks, the committee instead acted to alert the Petrograd garrison for the new insurrection, warning the soldiers to be ready to take arms against the Kerensky government in order to save the Revolution.

Time was now growing short, for on November 7 the Second All-Russian Congress of Soviets, with delegates from all over the country, was to meet in Petrograd. Lenin and Trotsky were determined to present the Congress with the Bolshevik insurrection as an accomplished fact, since they feared that the Bolshevik delegates would be in a minority. This was no time, they reasoned, for democratic procedures: the thing to do was to seize the power first and justify it afterward. Besides, they both believed that in a sense a Bolshevik revolution would be truly democratic, since it would aim to give the Russian people what very clearly they wanted: bread, peace, and land.

By the night of November 6, 1917, the Bolshevik camp was highly organized. Not only did Lenin and Trotsky have the promised support of most of the Petrograd garrison of troops, but in every big factory a unit of workers' militia—later famous as the Red Guard—was more or less trained, more or less armed with illegal rifles, and more or less ready to carry out specific duties in the insurrection. Special units had been designated to take over the telephone exchange, the railroad stations, the state bank, the printing plants, and the drawbridges spanning the Neva River. Whether each unit would carry out its revolutionary duty remained to be seen; but in any case, Trotsky, who did most of the planning, had thought of just about everything. Nothing could have made a more telling contrast with the March revolution, which had occurred haphazardly, without any planning whatsoever.

Nor could there have been a sharper contrast with the March revolution when the Bolsheviks' plans were actually put into effect, beginning about 2 A.M. on the morning of November 7. Instead of tumultuous street fighting, all went quietly, with ridiculous ease. In later years, when it was necessary for the sake of Soviet mythology to make the Bolshevik revolution sound as heroic as possible, stories of sharp encounters in the night, of fierce battles at particular buildings, and of daring exploits by individual insurrectionists were invented—but in reality there was very little of

A long-time Menshevik, Leon Trotsky (right) joined Lenin's Bolsheviks in the summer of 1917. The two radical leaders were determined to oust the liberal Provisional Government of Kerensky.

A post-revolutionary artist, glorifying Lenin's role in the uprising, depicted the familiar bearded figure outlining his plans to a group of fellow conspirators at a clandestine meeting. His wife, Krupskaya (left, background), an important revolutionary in her own right, sits by a samovar, awaiting a chance to serve them tea.

this sort of dramatic revolutionary activity at the time.

It was not that Kerensky's government had been unaware of the Bolsheviks' plan. The insurrection had been openly discussed for days before it took place, and even the timing was well known to the authorities. As a matter of fact, on November 5, in its meeting rooms at the Winter Palace, the government issued a number of anti-Bolshevik decrees: their papers were to be shut down; the Military Revolutionary Committee was to be arrested; the Smolny Institute (a former school for girls where the Soviet now met) was to be cut out of the city telephone system; troops were to be called in from outside the city. The only trouble, as Trotsky ironically observed, was that "in these formidable orders it was not indicated who was to carry them out or how."

There really was almost nobody to carry them out. The most reliable troops the government had on hand were the recently recruited Women's Battalion and the young cadets of the various military schools in Petrograd. Many of these valiantly tried to resist the Bolshevik rebellion, but with few exceptions they were ineffective—and no wonder, for they

Two fur-hatted officers inspect a troop of the Women's Battalion, under the watchful eye of the unit's commander, Madame Botchkareva (second from right). Formed largely of war widows, the group supported Kerensky's government.

were hopelessly outnumbered as well as, for the most part, hopelessly inexperienced.

By nightfall on November 7—a date that would become sacred in the annals of Communism*—nearly all of the city of Petrograd was in the hands of Bolshevik-led forces. There had been hardly any bloodletting at all, and some citizens were not even aware that a revolution was taking place. The streetcars continued to run as usual; most restaurants and shops were open for business; people even went to the opera and theatre just as if everything were perfectly normal.

Meanwhile, at the Smolny Institute, the members of the Petrograd Soviet—almost crowded out now by the arriving delegates to the All-Russian Congress of Soviets—were behaving as if talk were the essence of revolution rather than fighting. The brightly lighted building swarmed like an anthill. Outside in the courtyard dozens of autos and armored cars stood waiting, many with their motors run-

*According to the "Old Style" Julian calendar, the Bolshevik coup took place on October 25. This second revolution, now commemorated by the Communists on November 7, is sometimes called the October revolution.

ning as if they were impatient to be off to the scene of the action. Inside, the Bolshevik top command alternated between giving out bulletins on the latest successes of their forces throughout the city and arguing loudly with Mensheviks and Socialist Revolutionaries.

It was not until eleven o'clock on the night of November 7 that the Congress finally got under way. It was more of the same: talk, talk, talk. But before long the opponents of the Bolsheviks began to realize that all the talk would get them nowhere: events were passing them by. Most of them —Mensheviks and Socialist Revolutionaries, again—thereupon walked out of the Congress. At about 2:30 A.M. the chairman announced that the last stronghold of the Kerensky government, the Winter Palace, had fallen to the siege of Bolshevik soldiers and workers. After three more hours of excited talk the delegates, dead tired, voted in favor of a resolution stating that the Congress of Soviets itself would take over governmental power in Russia. Then everyone who had a bed to go to went to it, gratefully.

The "siege" of the Winter Palace, though it was the closest thing to a battle during the insurrection of November 7–8, had been something of a farce. Inside its ornate halls the ministers of the Kerensky government were protected by about two hundred military cadets, nervous members of the Women's Battalion, many stacks of rifles, and an enormous supply of fine wines that had been stored in the cellars in czarist times. Kerensky himself, seeking reliable troops, had hastily departed from the city that morning, escorted by an automobile borrowed from the American embassy and flying the American flag. (After unsuccessful attempts to rally Russian troops in his support, Kerensky returned in disguise to Petrograd. When the Bolsheviks ordered his arrest, he traveled to England and survived to become one of the most famous of Russian exiles. In 1967, at the age of eighty-six, he was still vigorous and living in New York City.)

The Bolshevik forces surrounding the Winter Palace on the night of November 7–8 were formidable. On the Neva the cruiser *Aurora*, whose sailors had come over to the new revolution almost to a man, was occasionally firing its heavy guns at the building. The guns were loaded, how-

Bolshevik soldiers surging through the arch leading to Petrograd's Winter Palace were painted in 1917 by E. B. Lintott. A modern photograph of the same view, framing Palace Square's monumental column, appears on page 6.

NIGHT OF REVOLUTION

Central Petrograd, on the night of November 7, 1917, was the stage setting for a drama that changed forever the history of the great Russian empire and of the entire world. That night, recreated here by an artist who has slightly altered the perspective to include all the historical sites, saw the overthrow of the Provisional Government by the Bolsheviks and the establishment of the first Communist state

CHARLES PICKARD, *Observer Magazine*, LONDON

Crowds, mostly peaceful, demonstrated or merely strolled up the capital's principal boulevard, Nevsky Prospekt (1) toward the imposing Admiralty (2). From his command post at the Smolny Institute (3), Lenin directed the revolutionary force that stormed through the War Ministry's arch (4) to Palace Square, dominated by a towering monolithic column. Their goal was the Winter Palace (5), former residence of the Czar and then headquarters of the Provisional Government. Guns from the cruiser *Aurora* (6) out in the Neva River and from the Fortress of Saints Peter and Paul (7), directed at the Winter Palace, also helped to overcome Kerensky's forces. A major scene of action in the March revolution was the Tauride Palace (8), meeting place of both the Imperial Duma and the rival Petrograd Soviet.

ever, with blanks in order to avoid destroying the palace unless it was considered necessary. Machine-gun detachments and infantry companies were strategically placed around all sides of the Winter Palace, and it looked as if only outright surrender would prevent a massacre if and when the Bolshevik forces attacked.

Eventually it was discovered that some of the doors to the building had been left unguarded, and a number of Bolsheviks infiltrated through them, wandering around the many corridors and halls, accosting the defenders and trying to argue them into surrender. In the end, the forces outside did rush the palace in a frontal attack, but by then the situation was so confused that, although there was much excitement, only six attackers were killed. There were no casualties among the defenders. The ministers of the Kerensky government were placed under arrest and taken off to the Fortress of Saints Peter and Paul; and the revolution— at least the Petrograd phase of it, which was the most important—was over. Moscow Bolsheviks timed their uprising to coincide with that of their Petrograd comrades, but bloody fighting raged in the ancient capital for a week, with a good deal of damage to historic buildings of the Kremlin. By that time, however, local soviets had wrested control of most other Russian cities from the Provisional Government.

The great event in Petrograd was ratified, in a manner of speaking, at the second session of the All-Russian Congress of Soviets, on the night of November 8. Lenin now appeared in the open, without his wig, and addressed the Congress. John Reed, an American reporter who was there, described the scene:

. . . a thundering wave of cheers announced the entrance of the presidium [the elected leaders of the Congress], with Lenin—the great Lenin—among them. A short, stocky figure, with a big head set down on his shoulders, bald and bulging. Little eyes, a snubbish nose, wide, generous mouth, and heavy chin; clean-shaven now, but already beginning to bristle with the well-known beard of his past and future . . . Now Lenin, gripping the edge of the reading stand, letting his little winking eyes travel over the crowd as he stood there waiting, apparently oblivious to the long-rolling ovation, which lasted several minutes. When it finished, he said simply, "We shall now proceed to construct the Socialist order!" Again that overwhelming human roar.

As for the first steps in constructing the socialist order, they consisted on that night of November 8 merely in voting to issue proclamations on three basic questions: the war, the

In the days following their sudden, almost unexpected take-over of the Russian capital, Bolshevik soldiers uneasily patrol the streets.

land, and the form of the new government. There were long discussions and debates—the session did not end until five o'clock in the morning—but Trotsky later very pithily summed up what the proclamations said on those three questions: "end the war, give the land to the people, establish a socialist dictatorship." That, for the moment, expressed the Bolshevik program, and even though many of the delegates to the Congress were not Bolsheviks, they apparently all were moved by the sweeping directness of it. At one point everybody stood and sang a funeral anthem, in memory of those who had fallen in the war, and the Internationale. N. N. Sukhanov, there as an observer, remembered later: "The whole presidium, headed by Lenin, was standing up and singing, with excited, exalted faces and blazing eyes. . . . the delegates were completely revived. . . . The masses were permeated by the faith that all would go well . . ."

The faith of the masses was going to be sorely tested during the oncoming months and years. Constructing the socialist order with acts rather than proclamations would prove to be a very difficult matter.

VII

THE BOLSHEVIKS IN POWER

"The day will come," the British statesman Sir Winston Churchill declared in 1953, "when it will be recognized without doubt throughout the civilized world that the strangling of Bolshevism at birth would have been an untold blessing to the human race."

In actuality, some strenuous efforts were made between 1918 and 1920 to do just that, by the British as well as by many others—including several thousand bewildered American soldiers who were placed under British command. Quite aside from those efforts (which will be described later), the conditions into which the "baby" was born were far from encouraging, and it sometimes seems a historical miracle that Russian Communism survived and grew. Its success can be attributed partly to luck, partly to the bungling of its enemies, and partly to sheer "guts" and brilliant improvising on the part of the Bolshevik leaders, especially Lenin.

Lenin, although he had an unquenchable inner flame of Marxist conviction, was above all a realist and a man of action. He said that beginning the Communist Revolution in Russia was "as easy as lifting a feather"; he knew only too well that to keep the Revolution alive would be more like moving a mountain. To do this, he was prepared to take any necessary steps, including self-contradiction, deliberate lies, suppression of civil liberties, forced labor, and cold-blooded killing.

Judged by the standards of right and wrong that most Americans believe in, the Bolshevik take-over of the Russian Revolution was an evil event. But Marxist standards of right and wrong rest on different assumptions. To under-

In the Communist propaganda poster opposite, a jaunty Lenin wields a sure broom to sweep from the globe such figures of the old order as kings, a black-robed priest, and—clutching his moneybag—a top-hatted capitalist.

stand how a man like Lenin viewed the Revolution, we have to consider what some of those assumptions are.

Marxism does not accept the idea of God. Since there is no God, the Marxist argues, there is no God-given set of moral laws or commandments that men—and governments —ought to obey. (After the Communists had made belief in Marxism one of the requirements for any public office, and even for getting into a Russian university, this joke was popular in Moscow: A student is asked by a professor, "What is God?" "God," says the student, "is a mistaken idea of the capitalistic class; there is no God." "Very good," says the professor; "you pass." "Thank God." the student exclaims.)

In the Marxist view, laws and customs are merely a reflection of the desires and interests of the ruling class: in a capitalist society, for instance, they reflect the desires and interests of the property owners, nothing more. On the other hand, the Marxist believes in determinism—that is, he believes that all events, past and future, are rigidly determined by laws of cause and effect that operate just as certainly in social relationships as they do in physics, chemistry, or biology. And just as biological evolution goes through a definite series of phases from "lower" forms of life to "higher," so human society goes through a series of evolutionary phases—also from "lower" to "higher." Essentially, for the Marxist, the evolutionary stages of society are feudalism (such as prevailed in Europe during the Middle Ages), capitalism (the present era's stage of individual ownership), and communism. Communism, since it is the "highest" form, is the system toward which all human society inevitably moves.

Note that this belief goes far to explain certain characteristics of Communists that often baffle non-Communists. It throws light on their stubborn, even fanatical insistence that in the end communism is bound to triumph and nothing can stop it. It also helps explain how a Communist can coolly commit what non-Communists consider to be terrible crimes: he believes that he is simply an instrument through which irresistible historical forces express themselves, and anything he does to help advance communism is therefore self-justified. Yet even though it is supposed to rest on scientific grounds, there is no way of proving that this belief in the inevitability of communism is valid: it really is a matter of faith—in a sense, a Marxist substitute for religion.

The Marxist theory of determinism, however, has another peculiar feature. The theory insists—again without

A candid photograph taken in Moscow shows Lenin and his sister, en route to a meeting of the All-Russian Congress of Soviets, walking past a building on which Bolshevik posters hang in tatters. A ladder leans against the wall.

any genuine scientific support—that human nature is fundamentally molded by the kind of economic system under which people happen to live. If they are factory owners under a capitalist system, for instance, they will have a set of beliefs and values that are quite different from those of the proletariat, or working class. By the same reasoning, in a communistic society, where the capitalist class has been eliminated and only the proletariat remains, everyone will have basically the same values and attitudes.

From the democratic point of view, this theory of economic determinism is the fatal flaw of Marxism, for it leads to a deadly conclusion. The conclusion is this: in a truly communistic world there could be no real conflict between the government and the people, for the government would *automatically* express the people's values. "Individual freedom" would therefore be meaningless. As a matter of fact, in some rather hazily distant future, Communist theory sees a utopian time of superdemocracy, when there will be no need for government in the ordinary sense. The people, all workers who jointly own all the material wealth of the world, will simply run things more or less instinctively, happily agreeing on everything of importance. This was what Lenin meant by a phrase he was fond of, "the with-

125

ЦАРСКИЕ ПОЛКИ

Пролетарии всех стран, соединяйтесь!

№ 35

ЗА ЧТО СРАЖАЛИСЬ ПРЕЖДЕ

"*Workers of the World, Unite!*" *proclaims a 1919 Soviet poster. Under the old order, at left, soldiers were asked to fight for a corrupt regime under Nicholas II. The vicious-looking Czar is flanked by Alexandra and Rasputin. At right, in sharp contrast, is the*

happy Communist state, in which soldiers, sailors, and peasants join in defense of a prosperous new land. In the background are the fertile fields, neat villages, towering cities, and busy factories of the utopian state Russia's new rulers were promising.

127

ering away of the state"—that is, of the government. "While there is a state," Lenin declared, "there is no freedom. When there is freedom, there will be no state."

There would have to be a transitional period, of course, and it was this period that Lenin and his fellow Bolsheviks believed they were entering after the success of their uprising on November 7, 1917. During the transition, the length of which it was not possible to predict, Russia would be ruled by what the Bolsheviks called the dictatorship of the proletariat. In theory this meant that the masses of "toilers" —the peasants, fishermen, miners, factory workers—would collectively act as a "dictator" in order to stamp out capitalism and resist any counterrevolutionary individuals or groups, whether inside or outside the country. In practice, since the masses were in an extremely unsettled condition, it meant that the local and regional soviets would run the country as they were directed to do by the All-Russian Congress of Soviets. The Central Executive Committee of the Congress in turn delegated actual governmental authority to the Council of People's Commissars, or Sovnarkom, as it was often called. Thus the power really flowed from the top of the pyramid down, even though in principle the people were the source of all power. Whatever Sovnarkom and the Bolshevik leaders decided to do, they could claim that their actions represented the "will of the people." This kind of thinking was used to justify a rigid censorship over all newspapers and books as part of the dictatorship of the proletariat.

Although he never lost his interest in theory, Lenin was much more concerned about practice during the tense and dangerous months following the Bolshevik *coup d'état*. He concentrated especially on three problems. First, if he and his group were to keep their hold on the government, they must see to it that the power of their opponents in Russian politics was reduced to little or nothing. At the same time, the Bolshevik leadership had to take steps to rally most of the Russian people to their program or at any rate satisfy them enough so that they would not actively oppose it. Third, the threat of the German army still hung over the country like a thundercloud, and something had to be done about that danger quickly.

The political problem arose immediately, for a national election—scheduled by the Kerensky government—was still slated for November 25. Its purpose was to choose delegates to a Constituent Assembly, which would debate the question of just what kind of society the new Russia ought to have. Inevitably the delegates would also debate whether or not to approve the Bolshevik government. The Bolsheviks dared not call off the election, which they knew had tremendous popular appeal; yet, just as they feared, they came out very much the underdogs when the votes were counted. Out of 707 delegates, only 175 were Bolsheviks. Leading the poll were the Socialist Revolutionaries, with over 400 delegates. Only about 40 of the SR's were far enough "left" in their views to be considered allies of the Bolsheviks.

In this embarrassing situation, Lenin caught his opponents off balance by agreeing to let a few Left SR's into Sovnarkom, thus forming a "coalition" government. When the Constituent Assembly met, on January 18, 1918, however, the Bolsheviks closed it down after a few hours. Outvoted, the Bolsheviks and Left SR's walked out of the Tauride Palace, where the Assembly was meeting. The armed guards the Bolsheviks had stationed at the palace then announced that they were "tired" and hustled the remaining delegates out of the building. Crowds gathered in Petrograd to protest the dissolution of the Assembly, but Bolshevik troops scattered them with rifle volleys. It was as harsh a suppression as any the Czar had ever used against the Duma. The Bolsheviks justified their action—to themselves, at least—by arguing that in this case the suppression was "for the people," not against them. The Constituent Assembly, they said, had been chosen on a basis that did not truly represent the proletarian masses and the peasants of Russia.

Despite these highhanded tactics, Lenin showed that he was very nimble when it came to rallying the greater part of the Russian people behind the new government. Marxist theory called for putting all the land immediately under national control. Instead, Lenin announced a policy whereby any peasant family had a right to the land they worked themselves and to the crops they harvested. Only the great landowners were to have their land taken away from them. The Bolshevik leaders also understood that if factories were to continue production without serious interruption, they would have to do so largely under the supervision of the owners and managers of the old capitalist regime. Therefore, they left most of the factories as they were for the time being, although committees of workers were to be chosen in each plant to supervise production. In other words, the Communist program was to be introduced very gradually. Lenin was always ready to compromise, at

Recording Lenin's role as founder of the Soviet state, a Russian artist depicted the Bolshevik leader explaining his ambitious plan for rural electrification (map in background) to an enrapt group of workers, peasants, and soldiers.

least temporarily, when he felt that it was in the Bolshevik interest to do so.

As for the war with Germany, the Bolshevik government was in no position to do anything *except* compromise, and that very drastically. Although he had to convince most of his colleagues, including Trotsky, Lenin insisted that an immediate peace treaty was necessary if the Bolshevik government was going to survive and begin to put its program into operation. A preliminary armistice with Ger-

many had been signed in mid-December, 1917, and peace negotiations opened toward the end of that month. After several weeks of bickering with the Central Powers, the Bolshevik delegation, headed by Trotsky, announced that it would not sign a peace treaty. Nor, Trotsky said to his astonished adversaries, would Russia continue to make war. The nation would simply withdraw from the front and demobilize its forces. The Germans promptly began a new advance against Russia on February 18, 1918, and were meeting with practically no resistance from Russian forces. It was obvious that they could push on to Petrograd and Moscow virtually unopposed. Under that threat the Bolsheviks unhappily signed a peace treaty at Brest-Litovsk, Poland, on March 3. The harsh treaty deprived Russia of huge chunks of territory (including Finland, Estonia, Latvia, Lithuania, Poland, and the Ukraine) and about one third of her population. Moreover, Russia lost one third of her farmlands, one half of her industries, and up to 90 per cent of such important resources as coal. What the Bolsheviks got in return was a chance to strengthen their control inside the territory left to them, without fear of German invasion.

Russia's new leaders had plenty of other worries. The Left SR's resigned from the government in protest against the treaty, but they continued to agitate against the Bolsheviks, sometimes only with words but sometimes with plots.

A less idealized picture of life in Russia during Lenin's rule is shown in the 1919 water color at right by Vladimirov: standing in the mud of a Petrograd alley, the poor root among garbage for food.

ANNE S. K. BROWN MILITARY COLLECTION

131

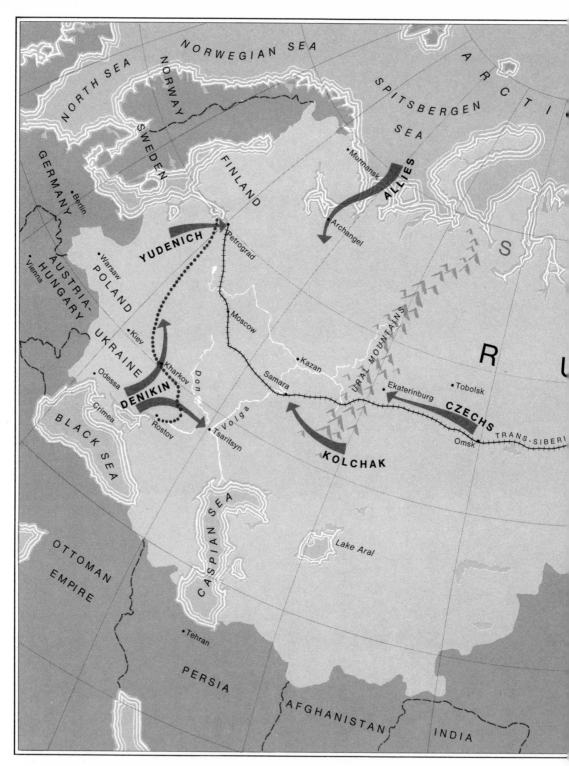

EMPIRE BESIEGED

The vast empire that Nicholas lost in March, 1917, and that Kerensky in turn lost to the Bolsheviks the following November, was besieged on all sides by mid-1918. Under terms of the Treaty of Brest-Litovsk, the Communists had been forced to surrender to German occu-

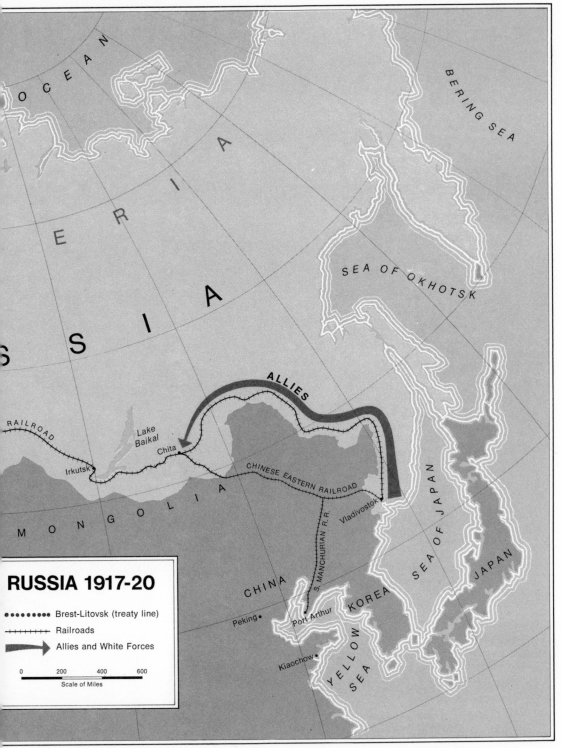

RUSSIA 1917-20

•••••••• Brest-Litovsk (treaty line)

++++++++ Railroads

Allies and White Forces

0   200   400   600

Scale of Miles

pation forces the heavily populated areas of Poland and the Ukraine. In vain attempts to keep Russia fighting against Germany by toppling the Bolsheviks, the World War I Allies landed forces in North Russia and Siberia during the summer of 1918. Earlier that year, the Czech Legion had controlled much of the vital Trans-Siberian Railroad. Through 1919, White leaders, such as Denikin, Kolchak, and Yudenich, pressed the Bolsheviks from every side —the first nearly taking the new capital of Moscow, the latter almost seizing Petrograd.

Looking strangely smug and satisfied, a fur-hatted Trotsky was photographed at Brest-Litovsk, Poland, as he arrived to sign a humiliating German peace treaty.

The spring and summer of 1918 were an exceptionally difficult period [Trotsky wrote later]. At moments there was the feeling that everything was slipping and crumbling. . . . The question arose whether there was in the exhausted, ruined, desperate country enough sap to support the new regime. . . . Everywhere conspiracies were festering. . . .

To combat conspiracies, the Bolsheviks set up a secret-police organization, called Cheka (an abbreviation of its Russian title), which soon proved to be just as fierce and possibly more efficient than any such organization under the czars. It was one of the ironies of the Russian Revolution that the man who directed the hundreds upon hundreds of executions without trial carried out by Cheka was F. E. Dzerzhinski, a Marxist idealist who formerly had spent much of his energy organizing relief for homeless and neglected children. Now he was like another person: ". . . counterrevolutionaries, spies, speculators, ruffians, hooligans, saboteurs and other parasites," he announced, ". . . *will be mercilessly shot by* [*Cheka's*] *detachments on the spot of the offense.*" This was the beginning of what came to be known as the Red Terror, and it had Lenin's full support as a necessary defense of the Revolution. "There has never been a single revolution and period of civil war without executions," he declared.

Meanwhile, the economic condition of Russia was rapidly degenerating. Czarist mismanagement and the terrible strains of the war had left the nation in bad shape at the time of the March revolution in the winter of 1917. The fumbling efforts of the Provisional Government under Kerensky had not improved matters. Now the Bolsheviks were in power, but Lenin's careful plans to avoid upsetting the economic applecart by too rapid an application of Communist principles were not enough to keep matters from growing still worse. By June of 1918, food supplies in the cities were frighteningly low: it was clear that many thousands of peasants must be hoarding their grain because they got so little in return for it. Factory production was also at a new low. Some of the government leaders were convinced that Lenin's reluctance to push ahead with nationalization of agriculture and industry was the cause of Soviet Russia's economic troubles. Now they got their chance to try to prove it.

A new policy, which came to be known as War Communism, decreed that all big factories would be taken over by the government, and along with this, all workers became subject to "labor conscription"—that is, they had to work where, when, and at what the government directed. To solve the food shortage, a "food army" was established, and contingents of armed men roamed the countryside, taking grain from the peasants by force when necessary. In March, 1918, the Bolshevik leaders had moved the capital from Petrograd, with all its czarist memories, to Russia's ancient capital of Moscow. About that time they also changed their official name to the Communist Party. Comparing the initial joy of the November revolution with the hardships that soon followed, confused peasants began complaining that the generous Bolsheviks had given them land but the cruel Communists were taking away from them the food they had grown on their new property.

In the long run, War Communism was not very successful and was eventually given up. It was unable to meet the emergency situation that had led to its introduction and for which it was named: civil war. Before the Bolsheviks came to power, about 45,000 Czechoslovak soldiers, most of them deserters from the Austrian army, had been formed into a corps to fight with Russia against Germany. After the Treaty of Brest-Litovsk took Russia out of the war, the Allies hatched a scheme to take the Czech troops around

Russia's uneducated peasants suffered most from the turmoil of revolution, enemy occupation, and civil war. The man in patchwork rags above and the aged woman below were among the era's refugees.

A bit self-conscious of his over-size fur hat, an American soldier poses stiffly in a snow-covered trench on the North Russia front.

the world to fight Germany on the Western Front. Train-loads of Czechs were sent along the great Trans-Siberian Railroad toward the Pacific port of Vladivostok. But the transit of so many foreign troops across Russian soil created tension, and a number of violent clashes broke out between the Czechs and local soviets. This led to a general uprising of the Czech troops, and by June, 1918, they were in control of several important parts of Siberia, as well as sections of the middle Volga River and Ural Mountain regions. Anti-Bolshevik Russians swarmed to their banner, and soon the government in Moscow realized that the tired Bolshevik forces would have to be revitalized to fight off this new threat. Trotsky, as War Commissar, took charge of the Red Army and immediately began to demonstrate surprising genius as a military organizer and leader. Nevertheless, he was obliged to draft his soldiers instead of relying on volun-teers as he originally had hoped to do.

To add to Trotsky's troubles, the Allies decided to inter-vene in Russia. They were naturally very unhappy that their German foe was no longer fighting on two fronts and hoped to revive the Eastern Front. Some Allied leaders argued that intervention was necessary to end the civil war by crushing the Bolsheviks and restoring a strong govern-ment that would continue fighting on their side. Early in August, a small British force landed at the north-ern port of Archangel, on the White Sea. The weak Bolshe-vik forces there hastily withdrew southward, with the British in pursuit. Early in September the British were joined by five thousand American troops, who had gone to Europe expecting to fight against Germany but now found themselves off on an adventure against the Communists that few of them understood. President Woodrow Wilson had dispatched the Americans with the understanding that they would be used only to guard military stores that the Allies had sent to Russia. They were put under the command of British generals, however; and with a good deal of encour-agement from David R. Francis, the American ambassador to Russia, the British sent the doughboys straight off to the fighting front.

The Americans were in northern Russia through the winter of 1918–19, and during that time they were the mainstay of the small Allied force opposing the Bolsheviks there. They were poorly equipped against the ferocious northern winter—temperatures often went to thirty below zero, or lower—and British efforts to use them against the Communist regime came to very little. Nevertheless, some

*Determined soldiers of the Czech Legion were photographed in open boxcars,
partly camouflaged with branches, as they began their epic journey on the
Trans-Siberian Railroad. They hoped to fight against Germany in France.*

ROMANOV CAPTIVES

In the summer of 1917, after some months of comfortable confinement at Tsarskoe Selo, Nicholas II and his family were removed to Tobolsk, Siberia. There the ex-Czar enjoyed sunning himself with his children on a barn roof (left) and studying at the dining room table that doubled as a desk (right). The Bolsheviks, taking over in November, provided rougher guards and less food for the captives, and in April, 1918, moved them to Ekaterinburg in the Urals. As anti-Bolsheviks moved westward, it seemed that the family might be freed and Nicholas restored to power. On July 16, however, Bolshevik guards took the family to a basement room (below) and shot and bayoneted to death all seven.

VICTOR ALEXANDROV, *End of the Romanovs*, © 1967 BY OPERA MUNDI

hard-fought encounters took place between American and Bolshevik troops, with a considerable number of casualties on both sides, thus poisoning the United States' relations with Russia's new regime for years to come. Meanwhile, the Japanese landed forces at Vladivostok in the summer of 1918, and the British, French, and Americans soon joined them in Siberia—more to prevent the Japanese from grabbing too much territory from Russia than to suppress the Bolsheviks.

From other directions the Communist regime faced more serious threats. The Czech forces quickly pushed westward, driving the Red troops before them. An ex-admiral of the czarist Navy, A. V. Kolchak, took command of some very large forces in Siberia, including remnants of the Czech corps, and launched a drive toward the Volga in March, 1919. In Estonia, General N. N. Yudenich gathered another anti-Bolshevik, or "White," army of about twenty thousand and came near to capturing Petrograd in the fall of 1919. In the south a large Cossack army under General A. I. Denikin continued to assault the Reds until the end of 1919, at one time driving within two hundred miles of Moscow. For a while it looked as if Denikin might succeed in overwhelming the Red armies opposing him,

A grisly memento of the civil war, the photograph below records the scene of a White lynching party. After hanging four Bolsheviks, the execution squad invites villagers to take a closer look at the gallows, from which two victims dangle. The bodies of two more Bolsheviks appear in the foreground.

CHARLES PHELPS CUSHING, NEW YORK

Above are three of the chief anti-Bolshevik leaders: General Yudenich (left), who nearly captured Petrograd; white-goateed General Denikin (center), who advanced on Moscow from the south; and Admiral Kolchak (right), leader of the White forces in Siberia.

link up with anti-Bolshevik forces in Siberia, and overthrow the Communists.

The Whites got much moral and material help from England, France, and the United States, who had forced Germany to sign an armistice ending World War I on November 11, 1918. Many Allied leaders (like Churchill) would have been extremely pleased to see the Bolshevik regime collapse. Yet none of the White armies managed to mount the final offensive that was needed to overcome Trotsky's Reds. The Bolsheviks did have two great advantages, even though they were sorely beset: they were at the center of the struggle, with shorter communication and supply lines; and they were defending the soil of "Mother Russia" against foreign invaders who did not pretend to match the claim of the Communists that this soil now belonged, quite literally, to the Russian people.

One by one, the White leaders were defeated. They failed to form a unified front against the Bolsheviks, and enough Allied support for their cause never materialized. By the end of ·1920, the civil war was over, and most of the foreign interventionists had withdrawn. The Communist leaders were free to face their many other difficulties without the fear that a military disaster might smash all their hopes and plans. The Russian Soviet Federated Socialist Republic, as it was by then called, had turned out to be a tough infant despite what appeared to be the serious birth defects of the world's first Communist state.

The domed, balding head of an intellectual; the piercing eyes of a visionary looking to the future; the jutting jaw of a determined realist—Lenin appears in this idealized portrait as the founder of the Soviet state.

VIII

LENIN'S LAST YEARS

When the Soviet government had managed to survive both the civil war with the White forces and the harassments of foreign intervention, it could be said that the Russian Revolution was over. To follow much further the fortunes of the Russian people under the Communist leadership would therefore go beyond the scope of this book. But although the Revolution itself was over, the future of Communism was still so uncertain in 1920 that a brief look at the events of the next three years is useful in order to show the direction in which Russia was moving. One way of tracing those events is to see them as they were reflected in the life of Lenin—for the famous Communist leader was to die early in 1924.

Even though Russia was still in desperate economic trouble in 1920, Lenin was bubbling with optimism. He thought things looked very promising for one of the great Marxist dreams: that the proletarian revolution would soon become world-wide. At a great meeting of international revolutionaries in Moscow in July, 1920—the Second Congress of the Communist International, as it was called—he outlined a system of tightly organized Communist parties in all western countries, in order to prepare for the world revolution. Only a year later, however, he was far less optimistic, for a severe economic depression had discouraged the working class in most countries. Typically, Lenin's reaction was to urge harder work by Communist organizers, so as to be ready when the right time came.

Meanwhile Lenin had to face some very painful problems in Soviet Russia itself. The iron rule of Communism, especially when it went along with empty stomachs and miserable living conditions, had not produced a happy people. Just how unhappy many of them were was shockingly suggested in March, 1921, when thousands of sailors at the great Kronstadt naval base, on the Baltic, openly rebelled against Communist authority. These men were no reactionaries—on the contrary, they had been among the most enthusiastic supporters of the new regime, and Trotsky once called them "the pride and ornament of the Revolution." Now they were grimly disillusioned by the way the workers and peasants had been treated under the "dictatorship of the proletariat," and they demanded more freedom: free elections, free speech, freedom of the press, free trade unions, and freedom of the peasants to harvest their land for their own benefit.

But Lenin, Trotsky, Stalin, and the other Communist leaders had no intention of allowing a new challenge to their power. In the Soviet press they denounced the Kronstadt demands as "counterrevolutionary." Then Trotsky moved sixty thousand Red Army troops to Kronstadt, and in a bloody attack lasting several days, overpowered the rebellious sailors. Thousands were killed in the fighting; hundreds more were executed later.

Ever the realist, Lenin recognized that the Kronstadt rebellion was a symptom of a sick society. In an effort to improve the living conditions of the Russian people and avoid further rebellions, he introduced his so-called New Economic Policy. Actually, the NEP was a retreat from War Communism to a system of economic production much more like that of modern capitalism. There was to be a good deal of private enterprise. Workers were to be paid on the basis of their productivity; peasants were to be allowed to keep surpluses and use them in exchange for manufactured goods. Private enterprises were allowed to coexist with socialized industries, and government control of the latter was relaxed. These measures succeeded fairly well in pulling Soviet society out of the economic swamp into which it had been sinking, even though a terrible famine struck the country in 1921 and 1922.

By this time Lenin was in bad health, although he was only in his early fifties. He had been seriously wounded by an assassination attempt in 1918 and further weakened by years of strenuous activity as the leader of the Communist Party and the Soviet nation. In his modest apartment and offices in Moscow's Kremlin he habitually worked sixteen hours a day, with excursions only to make speeches at public rallies, attend long committee meetings, or visit some new Communist factory or work project. The first of three paralytic strokes hit him in May, 1922, and from then on he was a fading figure in the Soviet government.

It appears that in the few months left to him Lenin spent much of his time reviewing in his mind the whole fantastic history of the Russian Revolution. He was concerned espe-

In one of the last photographs taken of the great Bolshevik leader, Lenin—the trace of a smile about his mouth—poses with the man who was soon to succeed him.

cially with the vision of an ideal communistic society that had moved him from the days of his youth. Only now did his elastic optimism lose its bounce: as his last writings indicate, he began to wonder whether the Soviet triumph had not in fact betrayed that vision by replacing the czarist autocracy with a huge "bureaucracy" that was equally suppressive of the interests of the common people. Far from "withering away," the government had steadily grown more ponderous, extending its totalitarian control over every aspect of the life of the individual.

Moreover, Lenin was bothered by the fact that among the other Bolshevik leaders he saw no one who struck him as having the ability to push toward the goals of the Revolution without, perhaps, making things worse instead of better. In Joseph Stalin, who seemed eager to inherit Lenin's mantle, he saw a man whose thirst for personal power was so great that it might threaten the whole future of Communism. In his last testament Lenin urged his followers to consider a means of removing Stalin from the important post he already held, that of General Secretary of the Communist Party. "Comrade Stalin . . . has concentrated in his own hands unbounded power," he warned, "and I am not sure whether he will always know how to use this power cautiously enough."

But Lenin died on January 21, 1924; and Stalin showed that he was too crafty and too firmly entrenched to be dislodged by anyone. Instead, he sooner or later got rid of most of his old Bolshevik friends and rivals—Trotsky, Kamenev, Zinoviev, and many others—by means of exile, "purge" trials and executions, or assassination. For the next three decades the fate of the Soviet nation would rest largely in the hands of this man, who was more ruthlessly bent than ever Lenin had been to industrialize and modernize Russia, regardless of the cost in lives and freedom.

During his lifetime, Lenin had always carefully avoided allowing any cult of hero worship to grow up around him; but in death he was unable to prevent it. Hundreds of thousands of Russians attended his elaborate funeral in Moscow. Afterward his body, skillfully embalmed, was placed on display like a religious relic in a granite mausoleum in the capital's vast Red Square. There it lies today, visited almost constantly by long lines of faithful Communist pilgrims. Under the protective glass the well-known face appears thoughtful, as if Lenin were still pondering how the Russian Revolution could have strayed so far from his hopeful dream of a classless utopia.

OVERLEAF: *Undeterred by a Moscow winter's bitter cold, Russian pilgrims to Lenin's tomb outside the Kremlin form a seemingly endless queue in silent Red Square.*

BRIAN BRAKE—MAGNUM

145

Following two truckloads of their comrades, Bolshevik soldiers dash across Petrograd's Palace Square during their successful November 7, 1917, attack on the Winter Palace headquarters of the Provisional Government.

ACKNOWLEDGMENTS

The Editors are particularly grateful for the assistance of Victor Louis in Moscow. In addition, they would like to thank the following individuals and organizations:

Anne S. K. Brown Military Collection, Providence, Rhode Island—Richard B. Harrington

Forbes Magazine, New York—Leonard Yablon

The Granger Collection, New York

Serge Hapougin, New York

Library of Congress, Washington, D.C.—Virginia Daiker, Milton Kaplan, Jerry Kearns

National Archives, Washington, D.C.—Dr. Richard Bauer

New York Public Library, Rare Book Division—Mrs. Maud Cole

Alexandre Tarsaidze, New York

Maps by Francis & Shaw, Inc.

FURTHER READING

Black, C. E., ed. *The Transformation of Russian Society*. OUP, 1961.

Carr, E. H., *The Bolshevik Revolution, 1917–1923*. 3 vols. New ed. Penguin, 1966.

Chamberlin, W. H., *The Russian Revolution, 1917–1921*. 2 vols. Macmillan, 1935.

Chernov, V. M., *The Great Russian Revolution*. Translated and abridged by P. E. Mosely. Yale UP, 1936.

Clarkson, J. D., *A History of Russia from the Ninth Century*. Longmans, 1962.

Daniels, R. V., *Red October*. New York: Scribner, 1967.

Fischer, L., *The Life of Lenin*. Weidenfeld & Nicolson, 1965.

Florinsky, M. T., *The End of the Russian Empire*. New York: Collier-Macmillan, 1962.

Katkov, G., *Russia, 1917: The February Revolution*. Longmans, 1967.

Kennan, G. F., *Soviet-American Relations, 1917–1920*. Vol. I: *Russia Leaves the War*. Faber, 1956. Vol. II: *The Decision to Intervene*. Faber, 1958.

Kerensky, A., *The Kerensky Memoirs: Russia and History's Turning Point*. Cassell, 1966.

Pares, B., *The Fall of the Russian Monarchy: A Study of the Evidence*. J. Cape, 1939.

Payne, R., *The Life and Death of Lenin*. W. H. Allen, 1964.

Reed, J., *Ten Days that Shook the World*. New ed. Penguin, 1966.

Sukhanov, N. N., *The Russian Revolution, 1917. A Personal Record*. 2 vols. OUP, 1955.

Trotsky, L., *The History of the Russian Revolution*. New impression. Gollancz, 1965.

INDEX

Boldface indicates pages on which maps or illustrations appear

A 1918 American visitor to Russia photographed refugees at Samara, where Bolsheviks clashed with White forces.

153

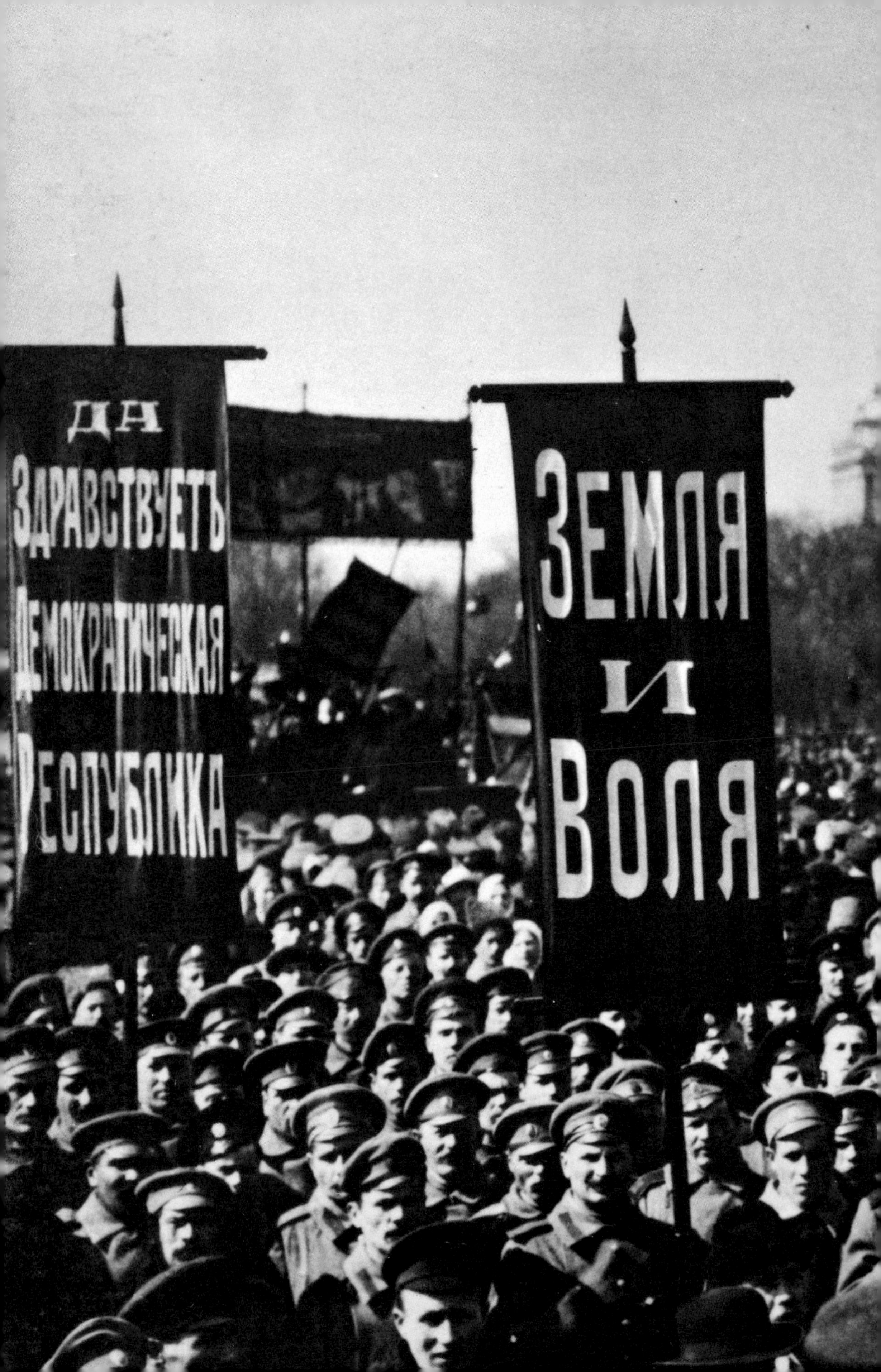
ДА
ЗДРАВСТВУЕТЪ
ДЕМОКРАТИЧЕСКАЯ
РЕСПУБЛИКА
ЗЕМЛЯ
И
ВОЛЯ